Praise for *Aging with Honor*

"For the 1-in-8 Americans in the 'Sandwich Generation' – Baby Boomers supporting their aging parents and their own children simultaneously – finances can get caught in the squeeze. This is why **Aging with Honor** offers significant help. Mark Schupbach and Jennifer Hicks have leveraged their combined 50 years of experience in financial planning to produce a workbook that walks readers step-by-step through retirement planning…from housing to healthcare, even to sensitive end-of-life decisions. Filled with sound stewardship, practical advice, and easy-to-follow worksheets, this indispensable guide provides financial protection and peace throughout each stage of retirement."

June Hunt
Founder, CEO of Hope for the Heart

"**Aging with Honor** calms the fears when navigating the turbulent waters of growing older. This comprehensive guide leads you through the difficult discussions and decisions of relationships, living arrangements, finances and more for parents and their adult children. It brings calm to help create a joyful lasting legacy."

Rob Pine
Executive Director, CEO of ChristianWorks for Children, Inc.
Vice Chairman, Board of Trustees of Christian Care Centers, Inc.

"My good friend, Mark Schupbach, has given us a much-needed, practical tool for developing and implementing a plan for us and our aging parents. In a unique way, Mark has combined his vast experience as a Christian businessman, financial planner and life coach to give us a clear, easy guide to follow on how to age with honor."

Lois I. Evans
First Lady of Oakcliff Bible Fellowship
Sr. VP & Founder of The Pastor's Wives Ministry, The Urban Alternative

"For those busily engaged with life's demands, the urgent overwhelms the important, the tertiary overcomes the primary, and the extraneous overpowers the essential in family, business and ministry. My wife, Bonnie, and I have found immense benefit in answering the questions and applying the directions of **Aging With Honor**, this manual couched in the service language of assisting the elderly among us."

Ramesh Richard PhD, ThD
President, RREACH
Professor, Dallas Theological Seminary

"Mark has made a major contribution to every family by authoring **Aging With Honor**. The succinct and pragmatic form of this book will support all of us in making the correct decisions about the aging process. Not only is the information vital to seniors and their family members, the worksheets allow the reader to personalize all 5 segments in this excellent publication."

Tom M. McDougal, DDS

AGING WITH
HONOR

Mark Schupbach
& Jennifer Hicks

ISBN: 978-0-9890230-0-9

Unless otherwise noted, all Scripture quotations are taken from the NET Bible.

Edited by Heather Jamison
Interior Design by Jennifer Hicks
Cover Design by Angeline Collier

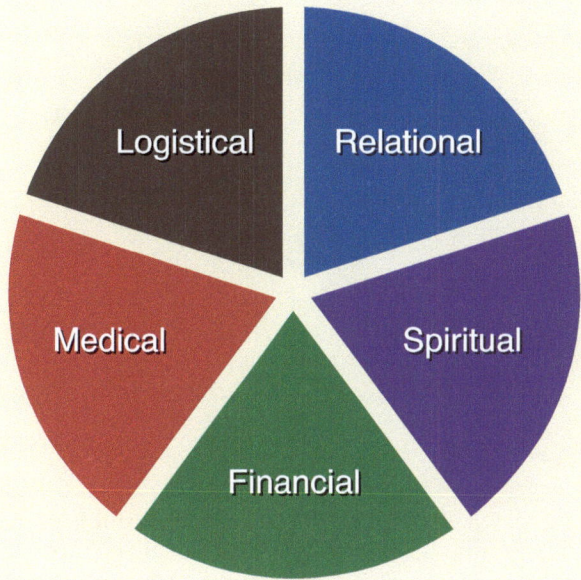

Logistical

Relational

Medical

Spiritual

Financial

AGING WITH

HONOR

Table of Contents

Mark Schupbach.
Believer. Husband. Father. Grandfather. Lay Leader. CEO. Board Member. Friend. Adviser. Connector. Problem Solver. Encourager. Visionary. Initiator. Supporter. Giver. Apple-geek.

Mark Schupbach is a businessman with a desire to use the experience, gifts, and talents he has been given by God to support and equip believers in their faith journey. He founded LifeMark Ministries to provide Christian life coaching and encourage believers to discover and implement their God-given purpose.

Mark's involvement with the church and ministry began more than 30 years ago. He has served as an elder and president on three church governing boards. He was also involved in Bible Study Fellowship for almost 20 years, including serving as the Men's Teaching Leader for 9 years. In 2003, Mark founded Next Step Bible Study to encourage participants to seek a deeper, more intimate relationship with the Lord Jesus Christ. Each week, over 200 people from over 40 different churches gather to study God's Word with a focus on practical application. With a firm reliance on the Holy Spirit, Mark enjoys exhorting believers to get out of their "comfort zone" and fulfill their purpose.

Professionally, Mark is the Founder and Chief Executive Officer of CPF Texas, a financial life-planning firm in Plano, Texas, that helps enable successful families to pursue their most important life goals. Clients benefit from his 40 years of financial experience in creative financial problem solving. He is especially adept at helping them draw out their values and prioritize their objectives. Believing that finances and faith are intertwined, Mark incorporates Biblical principles and values into financial planning and wealth management.

He received his undergraduate degree in business at Bethany College in Kansas. He also received the Chartered Financial Consultant (ChFC) and Chartered Life Underwriter (CLU) designations from the American College in Pennsylvania, and he holds FINRA Series 7, 24, and 63 securities registrations with LPL Financial. Mark is a Registered Representative with and securities are offered through LPL Financial, Member FINRA/SIPC. Financial planning services are offered through CPF Texas, a Registered Investment Advisor.

Mark has been married to his wife Marty since 1969. They have three daughters, three sons-in-law, and five grandchildren. They currently reside in Plano, Texas.

The following are some of the awards and boards that Mark has been blessed to be a part of over the last 35 years:
- *Hope for the Heart (June Hunt)*
- *The Turn Around Agenda (Dr. Tony Evans)*
- *EvanTell Ministries (Dr. Larry Moyer)*
- *Insight for Living (Dr. Chuck Swindoll)*
- *Dallas Theological Seminary - President's Council*
- *2012 Roaring Lambs Hall-of-Fame Honoree*
- *2010 America's Top 1000 Financial Advisors by Barron's Magazine*
- *2010 Bethany College Distinguished Alumni Award of Merit*
- *2007 Top 100 Independent Advisors in America by Registered Rep Magazine*

Jennifer Hicks has a diverse background in both business and ministry, and she enjoys using her experience to encourage others in their life journey. Jennifer received a Bachelor of Science in Applied Mathematics from Texas A&M University with an emphasis on Actuarial Science, and she holds FINRA Series 7 and 66 securities registrations with LPL Financial.

Working with Mark since 2007, she is grateful to God for opportunities to use her gifts and skill sets in a wide variety of projects.

One of her favorite things to do is spend the day behind a camera capturing the special moments of life as a freelance photographer. She is a die-hard Aggie, enjoys discussing current events, and is passionate about all things sports (especially Aggie football)!

❖ Preface ❖

I initially desired to write this workbook because I observed an increase in the needs of my clients for this information. More and more "Boomers" were coming to us saying they felt caught in the middle. Their kids were in college and expenses were rising rapidly, or they had recently graduated and were having difficulty finding a job. On the other side, the Boomers' parents were living longer than expected, needing professional care, and running out of funds. Our clients were looking to us for guidance on how to avoid spending their retirement funds just to make it through this stage of life.

Then about two years ago, these issues became personal in my own life. Both my father-in-law and my father had some health concerns arise and needed more hands-on care. We faced the need to make decisions about where they would live, if they could continue to drive, who would take care of them, and more. One lived out of town, so that complicated the issues as well. Suddenly, what I had been helping others through became very real for me. It confirmed that this workbook needed to be written so that others could prepare for this difficult time in life.

As we seek to **honor our parents** (or the seniors you are assisting), how can we best help them? My desire is that after working through this resource, you will be at peace with the preparation you'll have made and with the results when you carry out your plans. Many of the discussions and decisions are not easy, but creating plans now will give you more confidence and decrease your stress level down the road when the time comes to implement your plans.

We've spread the content out in this workbook in order to give you plenty of room to write in the margins, highlight important notes, tear out pages, etc. Use it! The more time and effort you put into preparing, the better. On the next page, you will find some interesting statistics we found in our research. Some of the statistics might surprise you. We have also provided additional tips and resources on our website: www.AgingWithHonor.org.

As with any project, there are many people who helped along the way. I'd like to thank my wife, Marty, for all the care and support she gave her father and continues to give my father as he ages. Her steady hand through this phase of life is such a blessing.

I'd like to thank my staff at CPF Texas, especially Jennifer Hicks for pulling it all together and bringing this workbook to fruition. Thanks also to Tom Knippa and Adam Spence for their contribution to this project and to Heather Jamison for editing and proofing the content. I appreciate all of you.

I sincerely hope that this workbook equips you to honor your parents as they age. Please feel free to contact us with feedback or suggestions on how we can better serve you.

Mark Schupbach

❖ By the Numbers ❖

Before we get started, consider the facts and statistics below that you might find interesting. [1]

- During the 20th century, the number of Americans under age 65 has tripled, but the number over age 65 has jumped by a factor of 11.

- From 1960 to 1994, the number of Americans over age 85 increased by 274% while the nation's population increased by only 45%.

- The life expectancy at birth has grown significantly over the years:

Year	Life Expectancy (in years)
1776	35
1900	47
1950	68
1991	76
2009	79 [2]

- Women generally live longer then men do, so elderly women outnumber elderly men in increasing ratios as they age:

Age Range	Ratio (women:men)
65-69	6:5
85+	5:2

- Over half of the population aged 85 or older who are not institutionalized need assistance performing everyday activities such as bathing, preparing meals, taking medications, and even simple things like getting dressed.

We have an aging population...who will take care of the elderly and honor them?

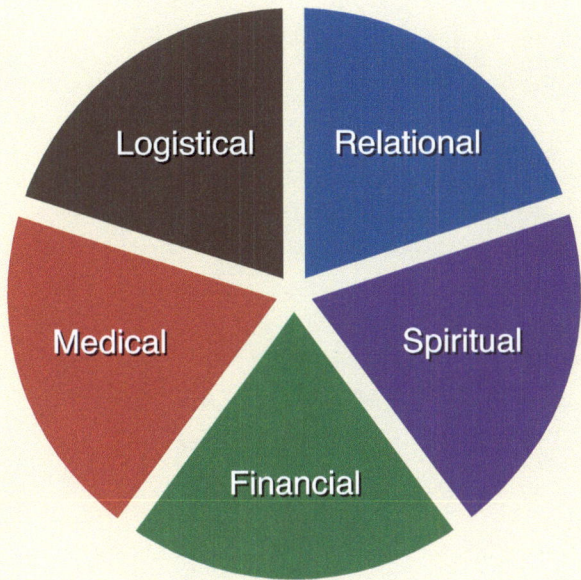

AGING WITH HONOR

Introduction

Congratulations! You are among a growing population of people who recognize the value of planning ahead -- whether you are reading this book in order to help yourself or a loved one, we hope the material presented here will equip and encourage you through the journey of growing older. Everyone's situation is different. There is no 'best way for all.' We will provide you with the groundwork to get started. For additional resources and tips, visit our website: www.AgingWithHonor.org.

This workbook will cover a variety of issues in five individual segments:

- Financial Needs
- Medical Needs
- Logistical Needs
- Relational Needs
- Spiritual Needs

This book is written to help adult children plan and prepare with their parents as they age. However, it can easily be used to help a grandparent, a friend, or even yourself. We will give you the tools and the resources that you need to evaluate your situation and create a plan that works best for your family.

Let's get started!

> *"Be proactive so others won't have to be reactive. The older generation should set an example of making important decisions while they are able to do so. Your children will someday be dealing with the same issues you are today. You can bless your children with the example of responsible planning."*
>
> Billy Graham [3]

❖ Why Planning Matters ❖

No one would consider leaving home on vacation without a map, an itinerary, and a plan for food, gas, and lodging as they head to their destination. There are numerous options and decisions that can be made ahead of time in order to afford the greatest opportunity to experience a fun and relaxing vacation. Having a plan is optimal in order to keep you on track.

Similarly, it has been said that many people spend more time each year planning their vacations than they spend planning their futures. Of course, nobody knows the future nor can they absolutely control all of the elements that comprise the future. However, most people agree that it is a smart thing to plan ahead.

So why don't more people do it?

Here are a few possible reasons:
1. It takes time.
2. It involves areas that you may not be familiar with or areas that you may feel uncertain about such as taxes, investments, or retirement plans.
3. If you are married, then you and your spouse may not agree on all of the decisions that need to be made so avoiding planning is somehow akin to attempting to avoid potential conflict.
4. It may force you to face some situations that you have created financially that could be unpleasant.

For these reasons and more, people will often delay setting a plan in place for their futures. As a result, they lose out on valuable time that is needed to prepare for retirement adequately.

Recently, there has been an additional issue that has come to the forefront with regard to planning for the future. This includes those who do plan, yet who only plan for the first portion of their retirement. This is the "fun" time which is spent traveling, playing golf, entertaining, and other things. What seems to be occurring is that little or no time and effort is being expended in planning for the second portion of retirement which is the more difficult time when people need to deal with declining health, housing needs, difficulties in performing everyday functions such as food shopping or driving, as well as the more significant end-of-life decisions.

Certainly, planning for the second portion of retirement is not an easy task. It takes a large portion of time and thought. In addition, most people will require assistance in order to plan successfully. There are numerous problems, difficulties and stresses which can make this a very difficult period. However, the benefits of proper planning are many and meaningful.

We commend you on initiating this very important process. The time you spend will take work, but we contend that it will be a labor of love as you assist your parents, relatives, or friends to plan for and live through what will hopefully be one of the most satisfying and rewarding stages of their lives.

✦ Action Plan ✦

As you go through this workbook, make a list of action items you want to take.

✓	To Do	Due Date
☐	Complete "Desired Lifestyle" for the "We" / "Me" Phases	
☐		
☐		
☐		
☐		
☐		
☐		
☐		
☐		
☐		
☐		
☐		
☐		
☐		

❖ Action Plan ❖

As you go through this workbook, make a list of action items you want to take.

✓	To Do	Due Date
☐		
☐		
☐		
☐		
☐		
☐		
☐		
☐		
☐		
☐		
☐		
☐		
☐		
☐		

Financial Needs

Since financial topics lay the foundation for all the other areas, it is important to start here. Finances will affect residence options, the level of care that is accessible, and even the financial legacy of the person or persons involved.

This workbook will cover a variety of issues that fall underneath the financial umbrella. These include:

- Desired Lifestyle
- Strategies for Lifelong Income
- Budgeting & Expenses
- Long-term Care Insurance
- Social Security
- Inflation Protection
- Avoiding Scams
- Passwords and Computer Logins
- Financial Legacy
- Financial Inventory
- Veteran's Benefit Programs

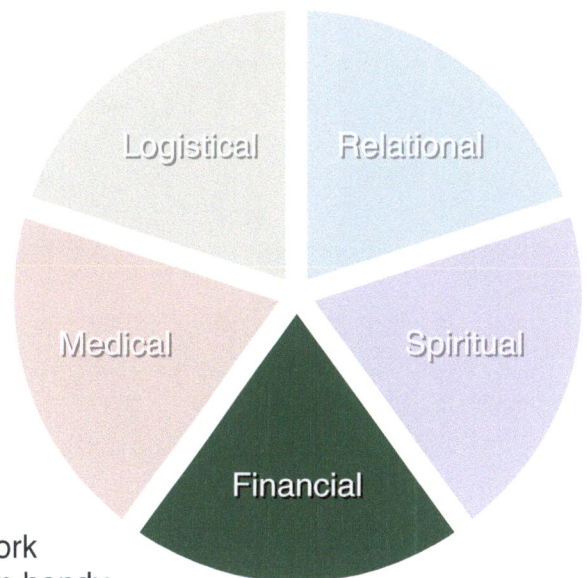

We will give you the tools and resources you need to evaluate your loved one's situation and lay the groundwork for future decisions. Make sure you keep the Action Plan handy as you work through this section.

Tips and Thoughts

To begin, let's take a minute to discuss a few things about the aging generation. Most people who belong to this generation are known for being both proud and private. This can be a good thing in a number of ways. However, it can also create a hesitancy within people from this generation to discuss financial issues with others. It would be wise to take the time to **earn the confidence of the person or persons you are working with** and **assure them of your confidentiality**.

> *The average annual cost of a nursing home stay is in excess of $73,000 per year and rising at the rate of 8-12 percent per annum.* [4]

Ask them what you are free to share with your siblings or relatives as well as what they want to remain confidential between you and them. Assure them that you do not want to invade their privacy, but that you are there to help them realize the importance of someone coming alongside of them to guide them in financial decisions as they age.

Desired Lifestyle

One of the major discussion points you should consider as you begin to look at the financial future of the person or persons you are assisting is the type of lifestyle they wish to maintain as they age. There are many options to consider. Keep in mind that the financial and medical situation of the person involved will greatly affect those options.

Take time to discuss the lifestyle preference desired. For example:
Is there a desire to travel? If so, where?
Are there any hobbies they want to learn?
What types of vehicles do they want to own?
Do they want to remain in their current home, or would they prefer to downsize to a patio home with less upkeep?
Would they like to move into a retirement community?

The goal of this discussion is discussion itself. It is important to get them talking so that you can ascertain what their dreams and goals are for their retirement years. It is vital at this stage not to give your opinion on whether something is a good plan or whether you feel like it is a bad plan. Be intentional about listening, and write down their comments on the following page.

If you are working with a married couple such as your parents, you will want to approach this discussion from two standpoints. During their 'We Phase,' record what their goals are for the two of them together. During their 'Me Phase,' write down the goals of each person individually should one of them outlive the other.

'We' Phase

'Me' Phase

'Me' Phase

Strategies for Lifelong Income

Income is important. It determines what options are available for lifestyle choices.

Most people focus on their account balances and return percentages because that is what they have done their whole lives. Their priority has been to accumulate.

As people grow older, however, they move from an accumulation phase to a distribution phase. As a person transitions into this phase, it is essential to transition the assets into reliable income streams. This involves a different way to invest and centers around both goals and plans, not balances.

There are many investment strategies used for generating potential income streams. It is important to 'stack' these in such a way that the timing is in line with your person or persons' goals.

It is time to evaluate their resources. Make a list below of their current and expected future income streams. List the amount and the start / stop times expected. If the income stream is dependent upon one parent remaining alive, make a note of that. For example, if a pension is only given for the life of the employee, that needs to be notated in case the situation arises where their spouse outlives them.

Income Source	Amount	Start Timeframe	Stop Timeframe

How do the income streams line up with their goals? If they are already retired or are planning to retire in the near future, you need to take into serious consideration how their portfolio should be adjusted.

Budgeting and Expenses

While it is true that 'it's all about income,' how people spend that income is also vital.

Take a minute to answer the following questions:

- How sure are you that the individuals involved have enough money to take care of themselves for the rest of their lives?

- Do they currently use a budget? If so, how well do they stick to it? Do they normally run out of money at the end of the month, break even, or have extra money?

- What large expenses are you anticipating for them in the next 3 years? In 4-10 years? In 10+ years?

There are several options for budgeting. The key is to find what works best for you and the individuals involved. In "Financial Worksheet 1: Budgeting" on page 10, you will see a system that we have found to work well for most people. It accounts for the regular expenses as well as the annual / periodic expenses in a person's life.

To implement this system, you will need two accounts - a checking account and a savings account. Fill in the income and expense information to determine how much should be put into each account each month that the income is paid.

Another good option is to use a computer-based program to keep track of your budget. You can use a software program such as Quicken or you can use an online option such as www.mint.com (tip: this is a free option).

When discussing budgets, make sure you pin them down on spending on grandchildren and gifts because these categories tend to be understated.

> "While caution is necessary when considering how to allocate your resources, don't become obsessed about your finances. Take control of your finances by setting up a sensible budget and sticking to it. This way you won't be a slave to debt, a victim of predators, or a prisoner of fear."
>
> Billy Graham [5]

It is also important that you not judge their spending choices. Try to help them account for their spending so that they have enough money to last, but keep in mind that how they spend it is up to them. Remember -- it is *their* money.

Worksheet 1: Budgeting

Monthly Income	"We"	"Me"
Social Security, etc.	$	$
Pension Income	$	$
Annuity Income	$	$
Other: _____	$ _____	$ _____
Total Monthly Income	$	$
	X 12	X 12
Total Annual Income	$	$

Monthly Cash Flow (Checking Acct)

Variable Cash Flow (Savings Acct)

Monthly Expenses	
Home Mortgage/Rent	$
Auto Payment/Gas	$
Maid	$
Yard Maintenance	$
Utilities	$
Phone & Cable	$
Home Alarm Service	$
Food - Grocery Store	$
Entertainment (Fun/Eating Out)	$
Charity/Donations	$
Health Ins and Prescriptions	$
Other: _____	$
Total Monthly Expenses	$
	X 12
Total Annual Expenses	$

Annual/Periodic Expenses	
Income Taxes	$
Property Taxes	$
Gifts: Christmas, Birthday, etc.	$
Home Maintenance	$
Auto Maintenance	$
Pest Control	$
Homeowner's Dues	$
Auto Insurance	$
Home Insurance	$
Life Insurance	$
Vacation/Travel	$
Clothing/Cleaning	$
Other: _____	$
Total Annual/Periodic Expenses	$

+

	Total Annual Expenses	$

=

Total Income	$	**-**	Total Expenses	$	**=**	$	Extra Cash

Long-term Care Insurance

What is long-term care?
Long-term care is a range of services and support systems that the individuals who are aging may need in order to meet their health or personal necessities over a long period of time. Most long-term care is not medical care, but rather assistance with the basic personal tasks of everyday life such as:
- Bathing
- Dressing
- Eating
- Transferring (to or from bed or chair)
- Using the toilet
- Caring for incontinence

What are the average expenses per month?
Care in a larger city is always more expensive than care in rural areas, but care in rural areas can be more difficult to find. Here are some samples of approximate expected costs in the state of Texas:
Assisted Living Facility = $3,091/month
Home Health Care Aide = $2,160/month
Nursing Home = $4,770/month [7]

Does health insurance or Medicare cover long-term care expenses?
Generally, Medicare does not pay for long-term care. In most cases, it will only cover expenses for medically necessary skilled nursing facilities or home health care, if you qualify. Medicare will not cover expenses associated with things such as dressing, bathing, food preparation, and the like.

> *Points to Ponder*
>
> - *By 2012, 75% of Americans over age 65 will require long-term care, and those costs are rising 6% annually. [6]*
>
> - *Increasing age is the greatest risk factor for Alzheimer's. Ten percent of individuals over age 65 are affected. This increases to nearly half of individuals over age 85. [6]*
>
> - *In 2002, approximately 26% of the adult population provided for a chronically ill, disabled, or aged family member or friend. [6]*

Methods of Paying for Long-term Care Expenses
Self-funding -- Most people with over $2 Million of investment assets choose to pay for their long-term care expenses out of their investment portfolios. Depending upon the total long-term care expenses, this can be a minor or a major drag on the portfolio.

Annual pay policies -- A number of insurance companies offer annual pay policies that cover long-term expenses. The downside is that if you never need the coverage, you lose the cost of the premiums.

Single pay policies -- This structure uses a single lump sum payment to provide for long-term care expenses but also provides a death benefit for your heirs if you do not ever need to pay for long-term care expenses. In addition, you have access to your lump sum payment if you wish to use those funds for other needs.

Worksheet 2: Insurance Inventory

Do you know what insurance policies the individual(s) you are helping have? Do you know what companies they are with? If something happened to one of them, would you know who to contact to get the funds? It is critical to sit down with them and fill out this inventory to organize their current insurance coverage. This will be helpful to you as they age. Also, take the time to verify that the beneficiaries are current on all life policies.

Life Insurance

Insurance Company Name: _____

Agent Name: _____   Phone #: _____

Address: _____

_____

Policy #: _____   Purchase Date: _____

Insured Name: _____   Beneficiary Name: _____

Death Benefit: $ _____   Cash Value: $ _____ (as of: __/__/__)

Premium Amount and Due Date: _____

Insurance Company Name: _____

Agent Name: _____   Phone #: _____

Address: _____

_____

Policy #: _____   Purchase Date: _____

Insured Name: _____   Beneficiary Name: _____

Death Benefit: $ _____   Cash Value: $ _____ (as of: __/__/__)

Premium Amount and Due Date: _____

Insurance Company Name: _____

Agent Name: _____   Phone #: _____

Address: _____

_____

Policy #: _____   Purchase Date: _____

Insured Name: _____   Beneficiary Name: _____

Death Benefit: $ _____   Cash Value: $ _____ (as of: __/__/__)

Premium Amount and Due Date: _____

Insurance Inventory

Home Insurance

Insurance Company Name: _____

Agent Name: _____   Phone #: _____

Address: _____

_____

Policy #: _____   Purchase Date: _____

Property Covered: _____

Premium Amount and Due Date: _____

Auto Insurance

Insurance Company Name: _____

Agent Name: _____   Phone #: _____

Address: _____

_____

Policy #: _____   Purchase Date: _____

Property Covered: _____

Premium Amount and Due Date: _____

Umbrella Insurance

Insurance Company Name: _____

Agent Name: _____   Phone #: _____

Address: _____

_____

Policy #: _____   Purchase Date: _____

Property Covered: _____

Premium Amount and Due Date: _____

Insurance Inventory

Health Insurance

Insurance Company Name: _____

Agent Name: _____   Phone #: _____

Address: _____

_____

Policy #: _____   Purchase Date: _____

Person Covered: _____

Premium Amount and Due Date: _____

Supplemental Health Insurance (if applicable)

Insurance Company Name: _____

Agent Name: _____   Phone #: _____

Address: _____

_____

Policy #: _____   Purchase Date: _____

Person Covered: _____

Premium Amount and Due Date: _____

Long-Term Care Insurance

Insurance Company Name: _____

Agent Name: _____   Phone #: _____

Address: _____

_____

Policy #: _____   Purchase Date: _____

Person Covered: _____

Premium Amount and Due Date: _____

Social Security

Full retirement age (the age at which you can begin receiving Social Security benefits) has historically been 65. However, because people are living longer than prior generations, Congress gradually raised the age beginning with people born in 1938 or later.

You will find the Social Security website to be very helpful in determining your full retirement age, calculating expected benefits, and even applying for benefits once you are eligible. You can visit their website for more details by going to:

www.ssa.gov

Inflation Protection

The key is to preserve wealth while still preserving purchasing power. It is a natural tendency for people to grow more conservative as they age, but investing too conservatively can hurt you because of inflation.

Losing your purchasing power is a risk that many people don't factor into their portfolio plans. Make sure you keep this in mind as you help those who are aging with their investment choices.

> *"Inflation is as violent as a mugger, as frightening as an armed robber and as deadly as a hit man."*
>
> Ronald Reagan [8]

Avoiding Scams

Another problem facing today's seniors is the number of scams that target their money. Unfortunately, they are prime targets for fraud, and it is easy for them to be lulled into giving away their information or even their permission to access their accounts. Educate the aging on how to recognize and avoid scams as best they can.

Listed below are a few tips to help you. For more information on how to protect yourself or someone you know, visit the following website:

www.fbi.gov/scams-safety/fraud/seniors

Here are a few tips to help the aging avoid becoming a target of fraud:

1) It is important to have someone they trust who is aware of their finances so that they are not taken advantage of as they grow older.

2) Have a good "allowance" system in place to prevent scammers from draining a large account once they gain access to it. In other words, only allow withdrawals up to a certain amount in an account before it gets flagged. Or keep a low balance in the account that they use on a regular basis.

3) Shred all outdated bills and documents that might contain private information.

Passwords and Computer Logins

As our world has become more technologically driven, our ways of accessing private information have changed. Password requirements have grown more stringent over the past few years as companies fight against hackers who want to steal personal identities. It is hard to remember all of the different passwords and security questions / answers, especially in the event that something happens to the individual(s) you are working with that prevents them from being able to tell you what they have already set up. For this reason, it is very important to fill out "Worksheet 3: Computer Logins" with them in order to keep track of this information. *Tip: Make sure this page is stored in a secure location such as a locked file cabinet or a home safe.*

Do your parents only use one password? If so, bear in mind that this is a dangerous practice. If a criminal somehow gained access to one of the accounts, they can easily gain access to the other accounts as well.

Here are some tips for creating strong passwords:

- It should be at least eight characters long.

- It should *not* contain your user name, your real name, or your company name.

- It should be a combination of uppercase letters, lowercase letters, and numbers. If it allows you to include symbols, that makes it even stronger.

Make sure they know that they should never send passwords by email, and they should never enter any personal information on a site that has been emailed to them via a link. For example, if they receive an email from what looks like their bank, tell them they should open a generic internet browser and directly type their bank's website address in the web address line. Once on their secure site, they can login and check the validity of the message. Never click on links in emails from unknown sources.

As an additional thought, if they enjoy using the computer to email or play games, you will want to find the simplest system available for them and then try not to change it. For example, touch technology can be easier for someone who is not tech-savvy to learn rather than using a mouse. Technological advances can be very difficult to manage. If the person or persons you are working alongside live in a location away from you, we recommend you set up remote access so that you can view their screen when they are having trouble in order to help them fix it.

Worksheet 3: Computer Logins

Date completed: _____/_____/_____

Phone/Website Logins

Company: _____ Pin: _____

Website/Phone #: _____

Username: _____ Password: _____

Security Q&A #1: _____

Security Q&A #2: _____

Security Q&A #3: _____

Company: _____ Pin: _____

Website/Phone #: _____

Username: _____ Password: _____

Security Q&A #1: _____

Security Q&A #2: _____

Security Q&A #3: _____

Company: _____ Pin: _____

Website/Phone #: _____

Username: _____ Password: _____

Security Q&A #1: _____

Security Q&A #2: _____

Security Q&A #3: _____

Computer Logins

Date completed: _____/_____/_____

Phone/Website Logins

Company: _____ Pin: _____

Website/Phone #: _____

Username: _____ Password: _____

Security Q&A #1: _____

Security Q&A #2: _____

Security Q&A #3: _____

Company: _____ Pin: _____

Website/Phone #: _____

Username: _____ Password: _____

Security Q&A #1: _____

Security Q&A #2: _____

Security Q&A #3: _____

Company: _____ Pin: _____

Website/Phone #: _____

Username: _____ Password: _____

Security Q&A #1: _____

Security Q&A #2: _____

Security Q&A #3: _____

Company: _____ Pin: _____

Website/Phone #: _____

Username: _____ Password: _____

Security Q&A #1: _____

Security Q&A #2: _____

Security Q&A #3: _____

Financial Legacy

This topic will be a tough subject to broach because most parents do not want to talk with their children about inheritance. Nonetheless, it is important that they think through the issues and speak with an expert to lay plans in place for the future.

Here are some things they should consider:

1) Regardless of the dollar amount that is left at your death, what percentages do you wish to leave to your children, your favorite charities, and the government?

2) Should the inheritance be left in a trust or with restrictions placed on it?

3) What happens to the estate should one parent predecease the other?

> *"Having your house in order is one of the most important things parents can do for their children. Give them the 'peace of mind' that you have your 'piece of mind' and have taken care of the business that has come about from your lifetime of labor. More than anything else, let them know where you stand with the Lord Jesus Christ, for this will be your lasting legacy."*
>
> Billy Graham [9]

There is no wrong answer to these questions. Your parents need to discuss their thoughts on inheritance and how it affects the next generation. Develop an estate plan that fits their financial legacy goals, and review it periodically to make sure it is current because estate tax laws change frequently. If your parents have considered the options prior to meeting with an attorney, it will save them time and money.

You can currently gift up to $13,000 to any individual in a year tax-free. That means that if you want to, you could gift $13,000 to your child and $13,000 to their spouse and reduce the size of your estate by $26,000 without paying any tax penalty.

Do your parents enjoy giving? Do they feel joy from seeing others benefit from their generosity? If so, encourage them that even though they should be wise about spending, it is okay (assuming they have enough funds) to give as they go rather than leaving it all in an estate to donate after they have passed away. This way they will experience the joy of giving.

Another important item to check is whether or not the life insurance beneficiaries are current. Most people do not realize that the beneficiary information listed on a life insurance policy takes precedence over information in their will. ***Verify that the beneficiaries on all of your parents' life insurance policies are as they want them.***

Worksheet 4: Financial Inventory

It is a good idea to take an inventory of all of the available assets as well as the liabilities. Having this information in one location is a great help in the event that the person or persons you are working alongside become incapacitated.

In the columns below, list all of the assets and liabilities as well as the current value of each. Include all their investment accounts, bank accounts, vehicles, homes, jewelry, credit cards, any valuable collections they have, and any other financial assets or liabilities they hold. Some samples have been filled in to help you.

Date completed: _____/_____/_____

Holding	Asset Value	Debt Value
Home	$350,000	$200,000
IRA	$250,000	0
Credit Card	0	$10,000

Veteran's Benefit Programs

If you are assisting a veteran and they meet certain financial qualifications, there are various programs that will help them financially as they age. Below are some of the more common programs and a list of resources to help you discover if they qualify for any of these benefits. Additional links and resources can be found on our website.

Veteran's Benefits
www.va.gov/geriatrics
www.northtexas.va.gov (if your parent is located in Texas)
www.nasvh.org/StateHomes/statedir.cfm
www2.va.gov/directory/guide/allstate.asp

Financial Needs Conclusion

This has been a lengthy section that has covered a wide variety of information. We applaud you for taking the time to go through it. You are doing great! Here are some of the things you should have accomplished by working through the Financial Needs section:

1) You know what lifestyle the senior or seniors you are assisting desire to have.

2) You have created a list of their income sources, amounts, and dates.

3) You have created a budget system that will work for them as well as for you.

4) You have researched the costs and benefits affiliated with long-term care insurance and have decided whether or not this is a good option for their situation.

5) You have made a list of their computer logins, passwords, and security Q & A's.

6) You have filled out the Financial Inventory worksheet and now have a good understanding of their overall financial picture.

Next, review the items on your Action Plan and complete any follow-up that is needed before moving on to the next section.

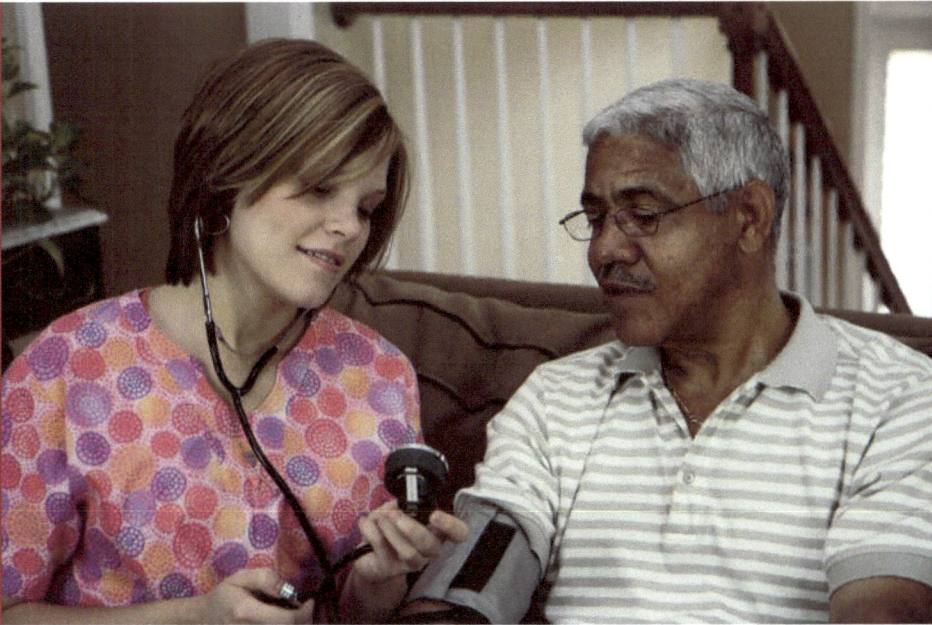

Medical Needs

Understanding a person's medical needs and options may seem overwhelming at first, but it is a very important topic to discuss because it affects many of the options available for residence decisions, level of care opportunities, and the like.

Keep in mind that this topic can be complicated, cumbersome, and constantly changing. The tips listed in this section are things of which to be aware; however, they are not comprehensive by any means. We will give you the tools and resources you need to evaluate the medical situation of the person or persons you are working alongside. We recommend that you find a local expert who is current in this industry.

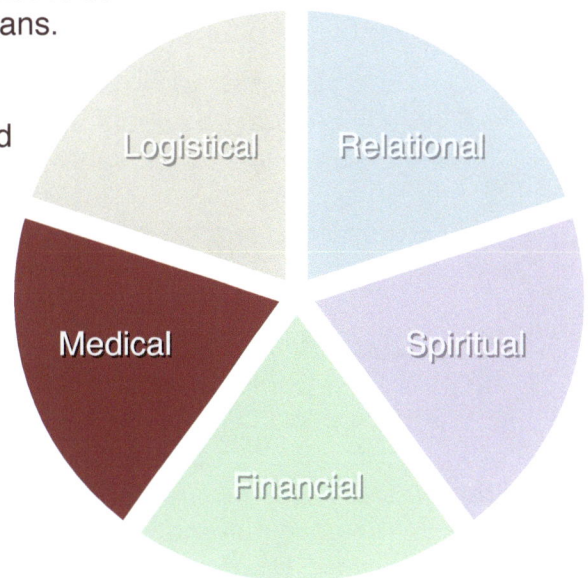

This workbook will cover a variety of issues that fall underneath the medical umbrella. These include:

- Medicare
- Medicaid
- Finding Doctors, Home Health, etc.
- Health Overview
- Health and Fitness
- Veteran's Health Care Benefits
- Hospice Care

Remember to keep your Action Plan nearby as you work through this section and write down any "to-do's" as you go along.

Medicare

Initially, Medicare can seem complicated and overwhelming. However, once you wade through the information and understand your options, it becomes easier over time. It is important that you walk through the options with those whom you are assisting. You don't have to be an expert, but try to learn the basics so that you can guide them through the process and make the best decisions together. In addition to the information in the next few pages, you can also visit our website for helpful links and articles.

Medicare is available for people 65 or older as well as people under 65 with certain disabilities or with end-stage renal disease (ESRD). Note that for Parts B and D coverage, you may have to pay late enrollment penalties if you decline coverage when first eligible.

Medicare has 4 components:
Part A - Hospital Insurance
- Partially covers inpatient care in hospitals.
- Partially covers skilled nursing facilities, hospices, and home health care.

> *"Everyone desires to live long, but no one would be old."*
>
> Abraham Lincoln [10]

Part B - Medical Insurance
- Partially covers doctors' services, hospital outpatient care, and home health care.
- Partially covers some preventative services for maintaining optimal health and preventing certain illnesses from becoming worse.

Part C - Medicare Advantage Plans (similar to an HMO or PPO)
- These are plans run by Medicare-approved private insurance companies and typically combine Part A and Part B under one umbrella. Some also offer Part D for an additional charge.

Part D - Prescription Drug Coverage
- Partially covers the cost of some prescription drugs.
- This plan is run by Medicare-approved private insurance companies.

Before progressing further, sit down with the seniors you are assisting and complete the "Medical Worksheet 1: Doctors and Medicare" found on page 28.

Signing up for Medicare:
If the person or persons whom you are working alongside are already receiving Social Security prior to age 65, then they will most likely be automatically enrolled for Part A & Part B of Medicare effective on the first day of the month that they turn 65. If their birthday falls on the first day of the month, then their coverage will start on the first day of the prior month. If they are automatically enrolled, they will receive the red, white, and blue Medicare card in the mail 3 months before their 65th birthday. If they don't want Part B, follow the instructions that come with the card, and send the card back. If they keep the card, they will stay enrolled in Part B and will pay Part B premiums.

If they are not automatically enrolled, they can apply for Medicare three months prior to turning 65. This allows time for paperwork to be processed, premiums to be paid, and Medicare cards to be distributed so that there won't be any delays in coverage. You can contact the Social Security offices at 1-800-772-1213 to enroll someone in Part A and/or Part B.

Seniors have up until 3 months after they turn 65 to enroll without a late enrollment penalty. If they elect not to sign up during their initial eligibility window, they can enroll each year between January 1 - March 31, and their coverage will begin on July 1 of that year. Note that they might have to pay a higher premium for late enrollment (read more below).

If they did not sign up for Part A and/or Part B when they were first eligible because they are covered under a group health plan based on current employment, they can sign up during the open enrollment period as follows:

1) Anytime that they or their spouse is working and they are covered by a group health plan through either the employer or the union (based on that work), OR

2) During the 8-month period that begins the month after the employment ends or the group health plan insurance based on current employment ends, whichever happens first.

It is important to note that COBRA and retiree health plans are **NOT** considered "coverage based on current employment." To avoid paying late enrollment penalties, make sure they sign up for Medicare when they are first eligible.

Medicare Supplemental Insurance (Medigap):
If they select to be covered by the Original Medicare Plan (Parts A & B) rather than the Medicare Advantage Plan (Part C), they will have the option of purchasing additional supplemental insurance called a "Medigap" policy. This insurance helps offset the costs that original Medicare does not cover like co-payments, coinsurance, and deductibles.

There is a common misunderstanding regarding Medicare payments that we will discuss briefly so that you will know how to read their statements accurately. Doctors will bill their regular fees, but they have an agreement with Medicare to not charge over a certain amount (varies by procedure). Thus, the "Medicare Approved" amount is the actual amount due, not the amount Medicare pays. Medicare will then pay a certain amount and those covered under Medicare are responsible for the difference between the "Medicare Approved" amount and the amount Medicare pays, regardless of the original amount that the doctor billed. To help offset these personal costs, many people purchase Medicare Supplemental Insurance.

Seniors have a 6-month Medigap Open Enrollment Period which starts the first month they are 65 AND enrolled in Part B. This period gives them a guaranteed right to buy any Medigap policy sold in their state regardless of their health status. Once this period starts, it cannot be delayed or replaced.

Every Medigap policy must follow Federal and State laws designed to protect seniors, and most insurance companies can sell them only a "standardized" policy identified in most states by letters A-N. All policies offer the same basic benefits but some offer additional benefits, so you can help them choose which one best meets their needs. *Note that Plans E, H, I, and J are no longer available to new enrollees, but if someone already has one of those policies, he or she can keep it.*

Important information to consider when purchasing a supplemental policy:

- What percentage will the premium increase annually? Does it increase on the plan anniversary (typically close to the birthday of the person covered) or on the calendar year?

- You will find that some supplemental carriers charge similar rates for identical plans but sometimes they do vary, especially in the expected future increases in premiums. Since the coverage is identical, it is worth shopping for the best possible premium from a company you trust.

- Below is a basic chart to help you understand *general* coverage levels of the standard policies. Each Medigap Plan covers the percentage of the benefit as follows (note that some of these plans do have deductibles so be careful in your selection):

Benefits per Plan	A	B	C	D	F	G	K	L	M	N
Medicare Part A Coinsurance and Hospital Costs (up to an additional 365 days after Medicare benefits are used)	100%	100%	100%	100%	100%	100%	100%	100%	100%	100%
Medicare Part B Coinsurance or Copayment	100%	100%	100%	100%	100%	100%	50%	75%	100%	100%
Blood (first 3 pints)	100%	100%	100%	100%	100%	100%	50%	75%		
Part A Hospice Care Coinsurance or Copayment	100%	100%	100%	100%	100%	100%	50%	75%	100%	100%
Skilled Nursing Facility Care Coinsurance			100%	100%	100%	100%	50%	75%	100%	100%
Medicare Part A Deductible		100%	100%	100%	100%	100%	50%	75%	50%	100%
Medicare Part B Deductible			100%		100%					
Medicare Part B Excess Charges					100%	100%				
Foreign Travel Emergency (up to plan limits)			100%	100%	100%	100%			100%	100%

Determining Whether or Not to Decline Part D Coverage Initially:

The person or persons you are assisting might be in relatively good health and on few, if any, prescriptions when they turn 65. If that is the case, they might be tempted to decline coverage initially and then join when they have the need. While they CAN do this, it is not always best to do it. Part of your job will be to help them weigh the options. We can also give you some guidance on this topic.

The late enrollment penalty is calculated by multiplying 1% of the 'national base beneficiary premium' ($31.17 in 2013) times the number of full, uncovered months the individual was eligible but did not join a Medicare drug plan and went without other creditable prescription drug coverage. This penalty is added to their MONTHLY premium for as long as they have a Medicare drug plan.

Here is an example to help you better understand:

Consider John who is 64 years old and in good health. He only takes one prescription that costs him $35 per month, and he is trying to determine whether or not he should decline Part D coverage of Medicare. Let's take a look at some hypothetical situations.

Option A: John turns 65 and declines coverage for 4 years but his health is starting to decline so he decides it is a good time to join at age 69. Assuming a national average premium of $35/month, he initially saved $1,680 by not paying the $35/month premium for 48 months. However, assuming he lives to be 85 years old, he will owe a late enrollment penalty for the next 16 years which will cost him approximately $3,225 by paying the penalty of $16.80/month for the next 16 years. This assumes the penalty & premium don't increase, but that is highly unlikely. If they do increase, the difference becomes even more drastic. So by thinking John was saving money, he actually lost approximately $1,545 by delaying his coverage.

Option B: John turns 65 and declines coverage for 4 years but has a sudden heart attack. He is now on several medications and decides to get coverage. Due to his declining health, John lives another 5 years to reach 74 years of age. In this scenario, John will have saved $1,680 just like he did in Option A. However, since he did not live as long after selecting coverage, his penalty was not as high. In this scenario, the late enrollment penalty would only cost him $1,008 ($16.80/month penalty for 5 years). Therefore, he saved $672 by delaying his coverage.

You need to consider the person's age, life expectancy, and overall health in order to help them choose what is best for them. It is also worth researching the cost savings they will receive under the drug plan. Even if they take a drug that is not covered by insurance, sometimes they will receive a special negotiated rate with the pharmacy because of agreements with your prescription drug company. If they save $15-20/month on the prescriptions, that can often off-set half or more of their monthly premium. By taking this perspective, they have coverage if something happens and they need additional medications; but because of the savings, their net cost is not quite as bad.

Worksheet 1: Doctors & Medicare

Call their current doctors and ask if they accept Original Medicare (Part A & Part B) and/or the Medicare Advantage Plans (Part C). **Many people find that their doctor does not accept the Advantage Plans, so be careful about this step.** Make a list of the doctors below and the answer of each as you call them. Depending on your situation, this could be a project that the senior could do once you coach them through the steps.

Also keep a copy of this list with your other important documents in case of emergency.

On the next page, you will see a chart to help you decide what is in the best interest of your loved one.

Doctor's Name	Phone Number	Accept Original Medicare?	Accept Medicare Advantage?
Primary Doctor:	( ) -		
Cardiologist:	( ) -		
Rheumatologist:	( ) -		
Endocrinologist:	( ) -		
Gastroenterologist:	( ) -		
Dermatologist:	( ) -		
Neurologist:	( ) -		
Pulmonologist:	( ) -		
Ophthalmologist:	( ) -		
Other:	( ) -		
Other:	( ) -		
Other:	( ) -		
Other:	( ) -		

Doctors & Medicare

After conferring with your doctors, which option works best for you? Work through the chart below to determine this.

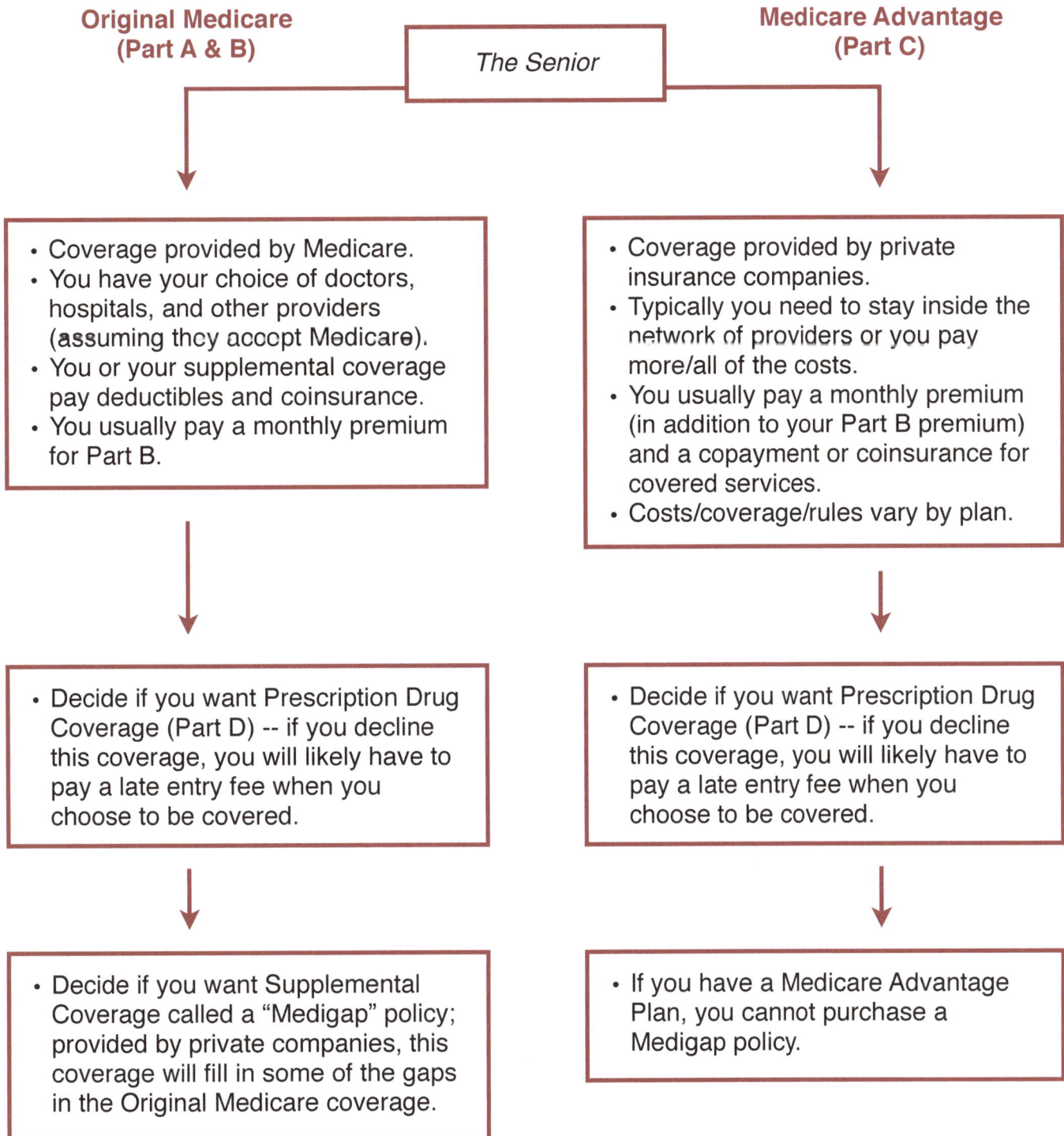

Original Medicare (Part A & B)

The Senior

Medicare Advantage (Part C)

- Coverage provided by Medicare.
- You have your choice of doctors, hospitals, and other providers (assuming they accept Medicare).
- You or your supplemental coverage pay deductibles and coinsurance.
- You usually pay a monthly premium for Part B.

- Coverage provided by private insurance companies.
- Typically you need to stay inside the network of providers or you pay more/all of the costs.
- You usually pay a monthly premium (in addition to your Part B premium) and a copayment or coinsurance for covered services.
- Costs/coverage/rules vary by plan.

- Decide if you want Prescription Drug Coverage (Part D) -- if you decline this coverage, you will likely have to pay a late entry fee when you choose to be covered.

- Decide if you want Prescription Drug Coverage (Part D) -- if you decline this coverage, you will likely have to pay a late entry fee when you choose to be covered.

- Decide if you want Supplemental Coverage called a "Medigap" policy; provided by private companies, this coverage will fill in some of the gaps in the Original Medicare coverage.

- If you have a Medicare Advantage Plan, you cannot purchase a Medigap policy.

Medicaid

A person 65 years of age or older who needs more than 30 days of continuous long-term care may be able to receive Medicaid if income and resource limits are met. The person must pay a portion of the cost by using all of his/her income, except for a small monthly allowance for personal needs and certain deductions such as health insurance premiums. The senior can also apply for payment of medical services that were received up to three months before the person applied for assistance.

The rules to qualify for Medicaid eligibility vary regularly and can be complicated. It is important to seek help from someone who has expertise in this area. To reach someone who can assist you, visit the Medicaid website and select your state in order to find your assigned Medicaid office: www.medicaid.gov

Finding Doctors and Home Health

Make sure the doctors of the person or persons you are assisting accept Medicare as well as any supplemental policy they have (if applicable). If you are unsure, you can contact their Medicare or insurance provider and ask them. If you need a home health provider for medical purposes, your doctor will be able to provide you with needed referrals. We will discuss non-medical home support needed (bathing, preparing food, and more) in the Logistical Needs section.

> *"You know you're getting old when all the names in your black book have M. D. after them."*
>
> Harrison Ford [12]

Also, if the senior is not yet on Medicare, make sure they have a primary care doctor and any other doctor you think they might need in the near future. This is because many practices will continue to care for someone who was a previous patient even after they go on Medicare, but they will not take **new** patients on Medicare. It is critical to plan accordingly.

It is also very important to consider the age of the senior's current and prospective doctors. If the doctor will be retiring in the next 10-15 years, the patient could get caught needing to find a new doctor when a large number of doctors do not accept new Medicare patients.

Health Overview

Sit down with the senior you are helping, and fill out "Worksheet 2: Your Health Overview." Keep a copy of it in your records as well as in their car, wallet, or purse.

It will also be helpful to have it readily accessible when they visit a new doctor's office or clinic, and it could be life-saving in the event of an emergency.

Worksheet 2: Your Health Overview

It is important to have a list of all current medications, medical history, and any allergies they have. You will find it helpful when they visit a new doctor's office or clinic, and it could be life-saving in the event of an emergency. *Keep a copy of this list with other important documents.* **It is also a good idea to keep a copy of this in your wallet or purse, or on your smartphone, as well as in the senior's wallet or purse. Update it as needed.**

Date completed: _____/_____/_____

Emergency Contact Names (& Relation)	Phone #

Allergy (Medicine, Food, etc.)	Severity/Reaction

Current Medication Name	Dosage

Brief Medical History, Surgeries, & Current Diagnosis

Health and Fitness

"If I rest more, I'll be able to conserve my energy for more important things."

"Working out won't extend my life a single day so why bother?"

"At this stage of life, exercising would do me more harm than good."

Sound familiar? You have probably heard your elders use these excuses to justify their lack of exercise. To be honest, we **ALL** use excuses of some form to justify our choice to not exercise as much as we should. Even so, it is vitally important to stress to seniors the importance of exercise in maintaining their health. Yes, as they age, they have to be more intentional in their exercise *methods*, but they still need to include some level of activity in their daily routine in order to have a more fulfilling lifestyle as they grow older.

> *"It is easier to maintain good health through proper exercise, diet, and emotional balance than to regain it once lost."*
>
> Dr. Kenneth Cooper [13]

Any health program for people over 50 should include a combination of stretching, aerobic activity, and strength training. Seniors should take proper care not to overdo themselves because it is easier to get injured as the body ages. Water activities like swimming are ideal because they put less pressure on the individual's bones and joints while still providing cardiovascular benefits.

Another great idea is to find a hobby that they enjoy which also incorporates exercise. Any sporting hobby would fit into this category assuming they are strong enough to play golf, tennis, or another sport. Even gardening can be a physical activity, as can painting, working with pottery, and other hobbies. Try to find something that interests them so they will be more inclined to continue it and even enjoy it.

Even if they are less mobile, there are still things they can do to maintain their strength and flexibility. In fact, there are several exercises they can do without even leaving their chair. Consider purchasing a DVD of chair exercises and encourage them to commit to doing them at least 4-5 times each week. They will see a difference in the way they feel.

Veteran's Health Care Benefits

If your parents qualify, they might be able to receive health care benefits through the VA system. Research the options for your parents on the VA website at: www.va.gov/health.

There are also links on our website to additional information regarding qualifications, coverage, and more.

Hospice Care

There may come a time when your parent's health has declined to the point that they no longer wish to continue health treatments. Hospice is a wonderful option to help people in the latter days. They bring comfort, both physical and emotional, to the patient and the family during a very difficult time.

Hospice care is provided to people who have a limited life expectancy and wish to spend their last months at home or in a home-like setting. The Medicare Hospice Benefit will cover the majority of Hospice expenses. If your parent does not have this coverage, some hospices will provide care using donations and gifts they receive.

> *"Let us touch the dying, the poor, the lonely and the unwanted according to the graces we have received and let us not be ashamed or slow to do the humble work."*
>
> Mother Teresa [14]

Note that not all hospice care is the same. Medicare requires certified hospices to provide a basic level of care, but the services themselves can vary among different Hospice providers. It is important to ask your parent's doctor, social worker, or friends who they recommend. Compare the options before selecting which provider is best for your family.

For more information, visit www.hospicenet.org.

Medical Needs Conclusion

As we said at the beginning of this section, medical needs can be overwhelming. However, you are making great strides in preparing for the future of those you are assisting by paying close attention to medical needs. Here is what you should have accomplished during this section:

1) You have a list of all the individual's doctors and their contact information.

2) You know whether or not their doctors accept Medicare and if so, which type.

3) You have researched the Medicare options and selected the one that works best for them.

4) You know whether or not they will qualify for any veteran's benefits.

5) You have completed the Health Overview Worksheet and made copies to keep in key locations.

Now review the items on your Action Plan and complete any follow-up that is needed before moving on to the next section.

Logistical Needs

Although it is not easy nor fun, it is important to organize logistical plans for the person or persons whom you are assisting. Whether that means determining where they will live, who will take care of them, or who has the authority to act on their behalf, having these items planned and organized ahead of time will greatly reduce the stress on everyone involved when the time comes.

This workbook will cover a variety of issues that fall underneath the logistical umbrella. These include:

- Personal Details
- Residence
- Driving
- Downsizing/Gifting Personal Items
- Professional Care Services (attorneys, taxes, paying bills, banking, and more)
- Personal Care Services (meals, cleaning, transportation, grooming, and more)
- Personal Care Options
- Interment Plans
- Lower-cost Burial Options
- Veteran's Flags
- Writing Obituaries

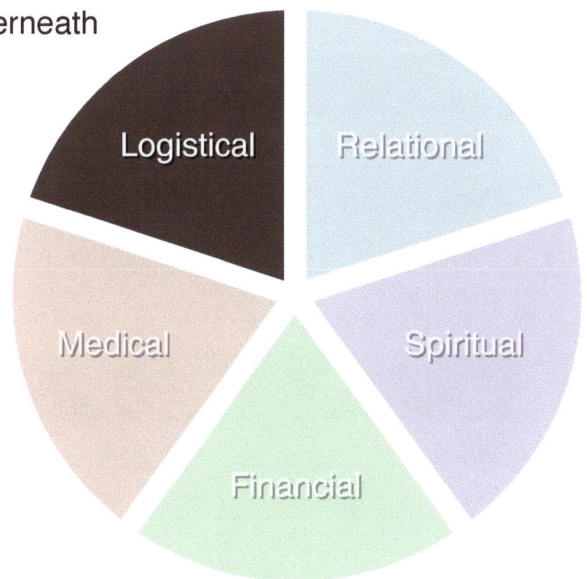

We will give you the tools and resources you need to evaluate the situation in order to make the best possible decisions. Should you require further assistance, please do not hesitate to visit our website. You will likely have several "To-Do's" in this section, so it is a good ideas to have your Action Plan on hand!

Worksheet 1: Personal Details

Before starting this section, sit down with the person or persons you are assisting to complete the following form. This will enable you to have this information should something happen to the individual. This is also helpful information to have in the event that you have to write the obituary. Make sure you have EACH person you are assisting fill this out with respect to their families (so if you are helping a married couple, make sure they each complete this form).

Personal Details
Your Full Name:
Current Address: _____   _____   # of Years at Current Address: _____   Prior Address: _____   _____

Date of Birth: _____
City, State of Birth: _____
County of Birth: _____
SSN #: _____
Citizenship: _____

> Attach a copy of your birth certificate as well as your marriage license and any other legal documents you think would be important to this form.

Your Father	Your Mother
Name: _____	Name: _____
Date of Birth: _____	Date of Birth: _____
Place of Birth: _____	Place of Birth: _____
SSN #: _____	SSN #: _____

Your Siblings	
Name: _____	Name: _____
Date of Birth: _____	Date of Birth: _____
Name: _____	Name: _____
Date of Birth: _____	Date of Birth: _____

Personal Details

Education

Name of School: _____   Date(s) Attended: _____

School Address: _____

_____

Degree: _____

Name of School: _____   Date(s) Attended: _____

School Address: _____

_____

Degree: _____

Military Service

Branch: _____

Serial Number: _____   Rank: _____

Enlistment Date: _____   Discharge Date: _____

Honors: _____

Fraternal, Service, and Social Memberships

Organization: _____   Organization: _____

Dates Active: _____   Dates Active: _____

Organization: _____   Organization: _____

Dates Active: _____   Dates Active: _____

Church Membership

Honors, Recognitions, and Misc. Notes

Residence

The residence conversation overlaps with the other topics in many ways. Most people want to stay in their home as long as possible, but it is better for you to use the language "as long as it makes sense." It is helpful to think through the alternatives ahead of time in order to decrease the stress and emotional strain that it can take on those you love.

Many types of needs affect the residence options. Are they currently able to maintain their home? Is the space overwhelming? Sometimes simply downsizing or modifying their home will extend their ability to stay independent longer.

You also need to take into consideration the financial resources available and personal care needs. We will discuss these items in greater detail in other sections of the workbook.

It is also very important to understand the emotional side of home ownership. For some people, it is where they grew up so it has a lot of memories attached to it. For others, it is a symbol of their independence. While it might not make practical sense to stay at the same residence, for many, the emotional toll of moving is simply too great. It is important to consider this when thinking through their options. Be patient with them and show them grace through this stressful process.

The Options

Your options will vary given your needs at the time. Within the options, the level of care varies greatly. The range of options include:

- Staying at current residence (with or without outside help)
- Downsizing
- Moving in with a relative
- Moving into a retirement community
- Moving into an assisted living facility
- Moving into a nursing care facility

> ## Points to Ponder
>
> • The majority of homes in America built before 1980 were not designed to accommodate the needs and accessories that often come with old age, such as wheelchairs or walkers. [13]
>
> • The average widow in the United States is 63 years old and is projected to live almost 20 years beyond the death of her spouse. [15]

Sit down and complete the "Logistical Worksheet 2: Residential" with the person or persons whom you are assisting. You might discover that they do not want to discuss this. If that is the case, try to approach it from a 'trigger event' perspective. 'Trigger events' are typically financial or health reasons that change the circumstances of a situation. For example, if mom mostly takes care of dad and he says it is working just fine and they will keep things just like they are, then ask him what if mom gets sick or dies before he does? What would be his residence preferences if that 'trigger event' were to happen?

Additionally, you will find some helpful resources in "Logistical Worksheet 3: Resources" to help research and implement the plan that works best for your parents.

Worksheet 2: Residential

Below are some questions to work through with the person or persons whom you are assisting as they consider their residence options and preferences.

Key Questions - Residential
1. What would your ideal living situation look like today?
2. What types of things would change your ideal living situation? (for example, death of a spouse, dementia/Alzheimer's, children or other caregivers moving away)
3. How would those changes impact your preferences? For example, if your spouse is the main caregiver and he/she passed away, would you prefer to hire a live-in assistant for 24/7 care (typically very expensive where available) or would you prefer to move into an assisted living facility? Or something else?
4. How close would you like to be to your family? If this involves moving, at what age or point in life would be the easiest/best time to make that transition?
5. Do you want your family to have full responsibility for your care? Do they have the availability, willingness, and financial resources to do that? If you plan on your family taking care of you, what steps can you take today to make that easier for them?

Worksheet 3: Resources

Below are some resources to help you determine what is best for the situation as well as to provide help to move forward with those plans, whether they need to modify their home so they can stay there longer or they need to move to an assisted living facility.

Home Modifications

National Association of Homebuilders
www.nahb.org/directory.aspx?sectionD=686&directoryID=188
This website will provide a directory of remodelers or contractors who have been trained in the unique needs of the older adult population including home modifications and remodeling projects.

National Resource Center on Supportive Housing and Home Modification
www.homemods.org
This website aggregates a collection of resources that promote aging in place and independent living.

Relocating to Housing Options that Provide More Care

Assisted Living Federation of America
www.alfa.org
This website will assist you in searching for a senior living community in your area.

Snap for Seniors
www.snapforseniors.com
This website compiles information from several living facilities as well as resources to help with aging at home.

A Place for Mom
www.aplaceformom.com
This company provides seniors free assistance to find the right housing choice for them. They are financially compensated by care communities nationwide.

Assisted Living
www.assistedliving.com
This company provides seniors free assistance to find the right housing choice for them. They are financially compensated by care communities nationwide.

Driving and Transportation

Deciding when your parent can no longer drive safely is very difficult and can often be the cause for ongoing conflict. It is important to listen to the senior involved and to try to give them as much independence as possible. However, their safety and the safety of those around them is critically important. Take into consideration if they live in a small town (which usually has slower speeds, easier navigation, familiarity with locations, and more forgiving drivers) or a large city (with lots of highway driving, faster speeds, and impatient drivers). It might work well to hire a driver or arrange regular transportation so that the senior safely maintains some independence and social contact.

If needed, you can involve the individual's personal doctor or optometrist / ophthalmologist. Sometimes they can speak to the individual in an authoritative way that they will accept. If necessary, you can request that the DMV perform a driving test.

Downsizing / Gifting Personal Items

It is important for the senior to make decisions about their personal items while they are alive, however small those items may seem to them now. It is amazing how many family arguments start over who gets the statue on the mantel that has no sentimental value, no financial value, and no one wanted it before the owner passed away. Suddenly siblings are squabbling over insignificant things and creating tension that is not necessary.

You can lessen this tension by encouraging the senior to give away his or her personal effects while they are alive. They can control the situation better plus they get to experience the joy of giving to those they love. There are several ways to go about doing this. Here are a couple of ideas you can suggest:

1) Instead of parents purchasing more things for you and your siblings as they age, ask them to give you things from their home. If they have strong opinions that they want to give a specific item to someone, encourage them to do it for their birthday or for Christmas. Or if they have certain things that would be really special to receive, you and your siblings could share those wishes with your parents if they are open to it.

2) If your parents aren't quite ready to part with an item but want it to go to someone specific at their death, they can put the person's name on the back/bottom of the item and explain to all of the siblings that the items marked are to be distributed as such prior to any other personal items being divided. This assumes they can trust their children to follow through with their wishes. If a specific item is particularly important to them, they should consider listing it in their will.

3) If your parent does not want to gift items during their lifetime, you and your siblings (if applicable) will have to divide items. You can draw numbers to take turns selecting, or you can make a list of your top items and try to work together so that everyone gets a few things they really want. You will have to choose the method that works best for your family dynamics.

Professional Care Services

Have the person or persons whom you are assisting created a will? If so, where do they keep it? Who has their Power of Attorney? These are questions you should have the answers to. If not, it can cause major problems as time goes on. Although it is not easy nor fun, it is important to organize their Professional Care resources. Too many families find themselves looking for the elusive 'lost' will. Or they have to go through the court system to obtain a power of attorney when they need to act quickly. Having these items taken care of in advance will greatly reduce the stress on your family when the time comes to enact your plans.

Solutions for these needs vary. An attorney can help with many of the issues including legal documents, estate planning, end-of-life healthcare decisions, and more. For other needs, you will want the assistance of professionals with expertise in that area. Below is a chart to direct you.

Professional Care Need	Provider
Wills/Testamentary Docs/End-of-Life Health Decisions	Attorney
Estate Planning	Attorney & Financial Advisor
Portfolio Management	Financial Advisor
Taxes, Bill Pay, Finances, Banking	CPA and/or Power of Attorney
Long-term Care Insurance	LTC Agent

If the will was made over 7-10 years ago or if there have been changes in the family (remarriage or birth / death of a beneficiary or death of an executor, etc.), then we highly recommend you arrange a meeting for the senior or seniors with an attorney. Along with wills, it is important that they have their wishes known regarding end-of-life health decisions. These are difficult decisions to be made, so most people delay this. In doing so, their wishes may not be known or honored when the time comes. No child wants to be in the position of making life and death choices for their parents so encourage them to take care of this now.

Sit down with them and complete "Logistical Worksheet 4: Professional Care" to help you think through their professional care needs and options.

Additionally, we have an Advisory Network of professionals whom we trust and recommend. If you are in need of professional care assistance in the Dallas - Fort Worth area, please visit our website for their contact information.

Worksheet 4: Professional Care

Below are some questions to work through as you consider the residence options and preferences of the individual you are assisting.

Key Questions - Professional Care
1. Do you have updated documents to address partial or total incapacity (including Durable Powers of Attorney, Medical Powers of Attorney, HIPAA Authorizations and Directives to Physicians)? If so, where are the originals kept and how might they be accessed if and when needed?
2. Have you updated your Will and/or Living Trust recently (within the last 5-10 years) to ensure that your current wishes are accurately addressed?
3. Have you built into your Will and/or Living Trust protection for your beneficiaries from creditors, divorced spouses, and eventual estate taxes?
4. What are your desires concerning life support in the event of a terminal condition? ...in the event of an irreversible condition that may linger for a long period of time?
5. Have you made provision for the possible cost of a nursing home stay or home health care? Do you have a long-term care policy? Do you understand that neither Medicare nor a Medicare Supplement Policy cover long-term care?

Professional Care

Have the person you are assisting help you fill out the following information, as applicable. This will provide you the information you will want to have in order to contact their advisors when the need arises.

Name	Contact Info
Attorney: _____ with Company: _____	Phone #: _____ Email: _____
Accountant: _____ with Company: _____	Phone #: _____ Email: _____
Financial Advisor: _____ with Company: _____	Phone #: _____ Email: _____
Banker: _____ with Company: _____	Phone #: _____ Email: _____

Do they have a safe-deposit box at a local bank or a safe in their home? If so, fill out the following information.

Box 1	Box 2
Location: _____ Address: _____ _____ Box #: _____ Keys: _____ Who has authorization to access the box? _____ What important items are stored here? _____ _____ _____ _____	Location: _____ Address: _____ _____ Box #: _____ Keys: _____ Who has authorization to access the box? _____ What important items are stored here? _____ _____ _____ _____

Personal Care Services

As your loved ones age, the need for personal care and services increases accordingly. If you or other family members live close-by, you may choose to assist them yourselves with transportation, meal preparation, house cleaning, and other tasks, or you may want to hire assistance.

Once you understand the level of care they need and want, you can narrow the field of care facilities. There is a wide-range of facilities available, and it is likely that they will use more than one while in various stages given their needs at the time.

The chart below will help you compare their needs with the level of care most appropriate for them, both now and in the future. Keep in mind that this chart is a generalized overview; specifics will vary at each individual facility.

Service	At home Services	Retirement Community	Assisted Living	Nursing Care
Meal Preparation	Available	Varies	Standard	Standard
Pet Care	Available	Varies	Not Available	Not Available
Lawn Care	Available	Varies	Standard	Standard
Basic Home Maintenance	Available	Varies	Standard	Standard
Shopping	Available	Varies	Varies	Not Available
Transportation	Available	Varies	Varies	Not Available
Personal Grooming	Available	Varies	Standard	Standard
Laundry	Available	Varies	Standard	Standard
Maid Service	Available	Varies	Standard	Standard
Basic Medical Care	Available	Varies	Standard	Standard
Advanced Medical Care	Not Available	Not Available	Varies	Standard

Personal Care Options

There are several resources that will meet the various personal needs your loved ones may have as they age. If they live in an Assisted Living Facility or a Nursing Care Facility, many of these will be included. However, they might need help with some of the services listed below while living independently. The list provided will help you begin this process, though this is a rapidly changing field so there are new services developing regularly.

In addition to these services, "Simply Home" is a good resource for security and monitoring services. Their website is www.simply-home.com and it explains the various levels of monitoring available.

Service	Comfort Keepers	Visiting Angels	Professional Caretakers
Website	www.comfortkeepers.com	www.visitingangels.com	www.professionalcaretakers.com
Meal Preparation	✦	✦	✦
Lawn/Home Maint.			
Security/Monitoring	✦		
Shopping/Errands	✦	✦	✦
Transportation	✦	✦	✦
Personal Grooming	✦	✦	✦
Laundry	✦		
Light Housekeeping	✦	✦	✦
Medication Reminders	✦		✦
24-hr Monitoring Care	✦	✦	✦
Respite Care	✦	✦	✦
Dementia Care	✦	✦	✦
End-of-Life Care	✦		

The service providers listed above are not affiliated with, nor endorsed by, LifeMark Ministries, CPF Texas, or LPL Financial.

Interment Plans

We plan for many of life's most important events: our wedding, our first home, the birth of our children, family vacations, and retirement. We plan ahead so that we can anticipate our family's needs and make sure all of the details are handled.

Then why do so many people leave such a significant event to their loved ones to plan during a time of sadness and distress? Doesn't it make sense to plan your funeral and cemetery arrangements ahead of time so that your family won't have to do so? Encourage your loved ones to talk through these choices now.

If they have already made arrangements, have they discussed them with the family? Have they shared with you any specific desires they have for a funeral service (specific quotes, pictures, songs, scriptures, etc.)? These are difficult conversations to have, but they are important. When the time comes to implement these plans, your family will be so relieved to not have the additional burden of determining these details.

Try taking the approach that you are trying to determine your own plans so that you do not burden your children (or possibly your parents if they outlive you!). Get your loved one's feedback on your plans and maybe that will open the door to discuss their preferences and desires.

"Worksheet 5: Interment Plans" (on the next page) will walk you through a lot of these decisions. Complete a copy for each of the individuals you are assisting because they will likely die at different times and have different burial wishes. It is also a good idea to complete one for you at the same time you are going through this process with others. Review these plans periodically as people sometimes change their minds regarding burial arrangements.

Lower-cost Burial Options

Some 'teaching hospitals' offer a service that allows you to donate the body of the deceased for organ harvesting and medical research. They will take care of all of the details and will cremate the body and give you the remains. If this is an option that your loved ones are interested in, call their local hospitals to see if this service is available in their area.

There are also coffin rental services if you plan to cremate after a funeral or viewing. Ask their funeral home if they offer this service.

Worksheet 5: Interment Plans

Fill out the following form with your loved ones to help them document their funeral and burial preferences.

Funeral Home/Burial Preferences
Name & Address of funeral home you have already made arrangements with (or if you have not made the arrangements but would like your family to use a specific funeral home):   If you have a pre-purchased lot, describe the location (i.e. lot #, block #, etc.); also, include a copy of the lot contract with this paperwork.
Do you have a specific contact at the funeral home your family should ask to speak with? If so, who?
Do you have a preference for viewing?   ☐ Open Casket   ☐ Closed Casket   ☐ No preference
Do you have a preference for burial?   ☐ Cremation - ashes given to family   ☐ Cremation - ashes scattered in the following location: _____   ☐ Cremation - ashes buried in the following location: _____   ☐ Traditional casket below ground in the following location: _____   ☐ Traditional casket in mausoleum in the following location: _____
Do you have any special requests for your burial? (for example, specific clothing or a personal item you would like buried with you?)

Interment Plans

Funeral/Memorial Service Preferences
Name & Address of church or funeral home you have already made arrangements with (or if you have not made the arrangements but would like your family to use a specific church and/or funeral home):
Do you have a specific contact or pastor your family should ask to speak with? If so, who?
Do you have any specific requests for your service? i.e. song selection, scriptures to be read, a specific person you would like to speak or sing or give a eulogy?
Make a list of pall bearers you would like to have if they are able to serve: _____ _____ _____ _____ _____ _____
Would you like flowers? ☐ Yes   ☐ No If not, then where would you like donations to be made in memorial?
These are my wishes as of _____ (date). _____ _____ Signature   Printed Name

Veterans Flags

If your loved one served in the military, you can request a flag to drape the casket or accompany the urn of the deceased. Visit our website to download the form or go to www.va.gov for more information. If the deceased qualifies, you might also be able to request reimbursement for up to $300 for burial and funeral expenses and up to $300 for plot-interment allowance.

Writing Obituaries

This can be a very difficult thing to do, especially in the middle of the grieving process. Some of the information you will need is listed in the "Personal Details Worksheet" at the beginning of this section. In addition, you may wish to write a more detailed or personal story about your parents in the obituary. We have listed several resources on our website to help you.

Logistical Needs Conclusion

You have made it through another lengthy, yet important, section. You are doing so well and should feel a sense of satisfaction as you put plans in place for the future. Here is what you should have accomplished in this section:

1) You have filled out the Personal Details worksheet for each individual.

2) You have discussed residence options and made notes regarding desired choices assuming various 'Trigger Events.'

3) You have discussed what 'Triggering Events' might affect driving abilities and discussed alternate plans for transportation.

4) Your loved ones have thought through how they plan to distribute their personal belongings.

5) Your loved ones have created legal documents and have an estate plan completed (if necessary).

6) You have discussed Interment Plans with them and have written down their wishes and had them sign it. You have helped them make accommodations accordingly.

Now review the items on your Action Plan and complete any follow-up that is needed before moving on to the next section.

Relational Needs

Taking care of the financial, medical, and logistical planning needs allows your family to focus more on the relational needs that arise as your loved ones age. It is a difficult time in life, and it is important to work together to achieve their goals.

This workbook will cover a variety of issues that fall underneath the relational umbrella. These include:

- Personal Legacy
- Family Relationships
- Restoring Relationships
- Family Heritage
- Losing Friends and Loved Ones

We will give you the tools and resources that you need to evaluate your situation, and if you need additional help, please feel free to visit our website.

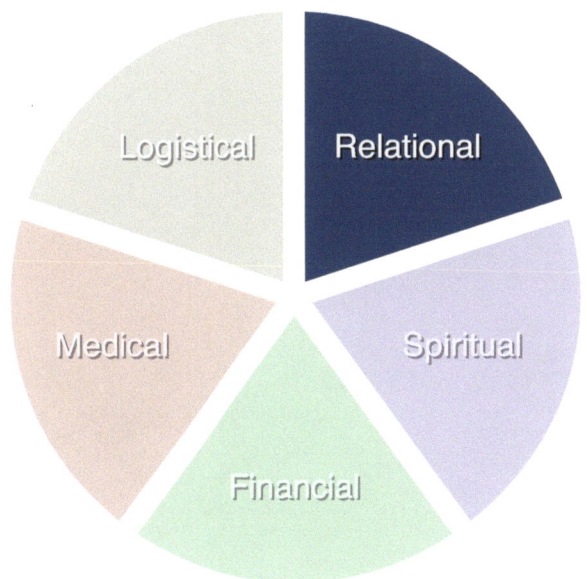

Personal Legacy

Sit down with the person or persons whom you are assisting and ask them questions such as: "What will be said about you after you have passed away? Whose lives have you changed? Where have you left an impact on the next generation?"

These are important questions that should be evaluated early enough in life to make changes if a person is not satisfied with his or her answers. It is never too late.

Start with an exercise to help them evaluate their influence. In the space below, have them write in the names of people or organizations who fit within each category.

For example, your *Inner Circle* might list the person's spouse, parents, children, siblings, best friend, mentor, or other person who plays a prominent role in his or her life.

In the *Middle Circle*, write in the names of people he or she comes in contact with on a regular basis. He or she should know these people by name but not be so personally connected that they would fall into the "Inner Circle" list.

Finally, in the *Outer Circle*, list the organizations or groups of people he or she impacts indirectly. This could include non-profit organizations they work with, groups they volunteer for, missionaries they support, departments at their company, social clubs, and more.

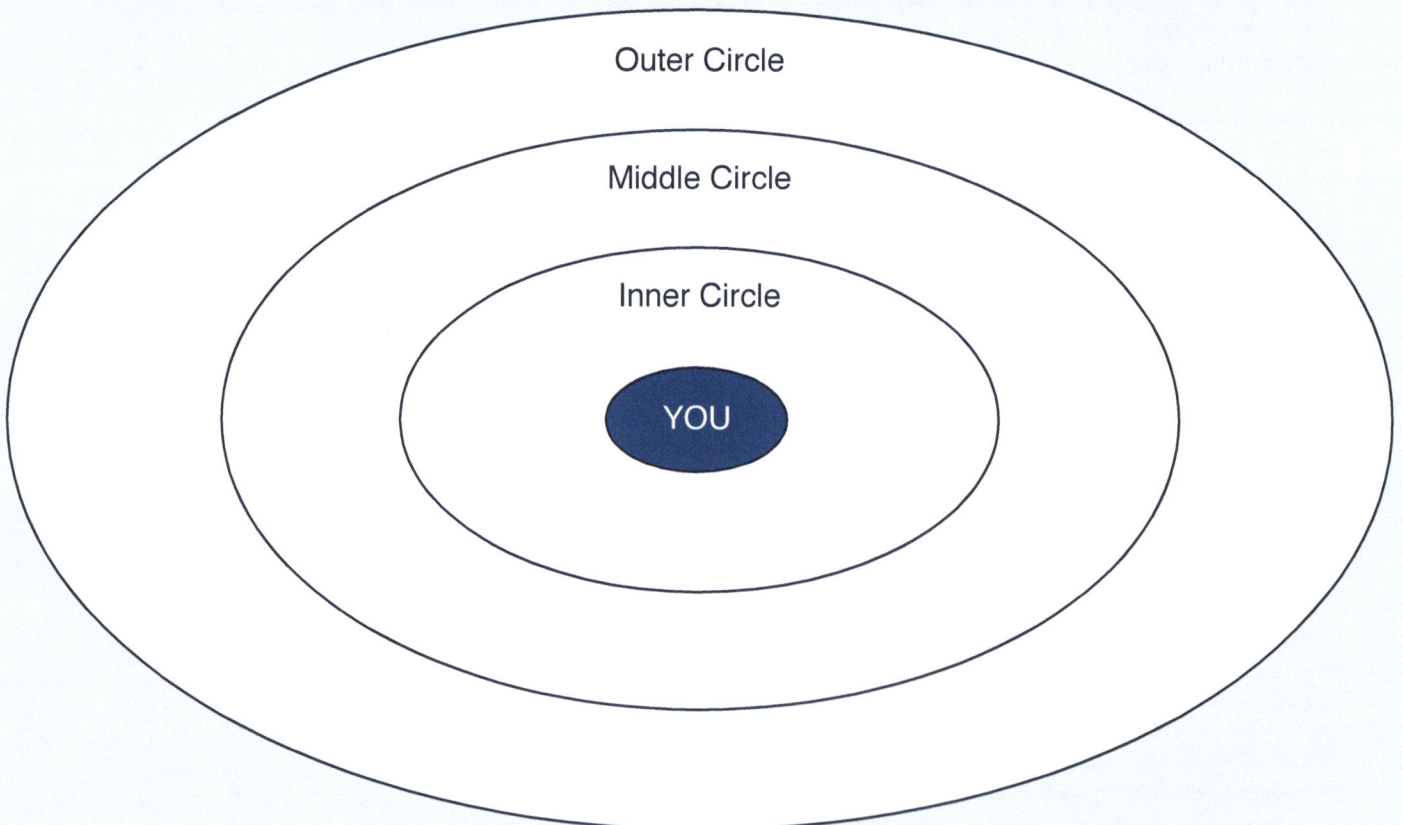

Outer Circle

Middle Circle

Inner Circle

YOU

Next have the individual think through the people in each of the circles. What impact is he or she leaving for them? Are there things he or she wants to teach them? Stories to tell them? Wisdom to pass along? Perhaps there are not many people / groups listed in the Outer Circle and the individual would like to change that. Encourage the individual not to procrastinate on these lifestyle changes. None of us are promised tomorrow, so the commitment to leaving a lasting personal legacy should begin today. *No one should squander the opportunities to change the lives around them.*

Below is a tool to help you apply this. In the first column, have the individual list the name of the person or group they want to impact. In the second column, list an action item that describes how they can implement the legacy they want to have. Be as *specific* as possible -- and *include the timeframe* they want to commit to. In the third column, list the date they want to start this action item. *Don't procrastinate, but be realistic.* Encourage them that although they won't be able to make all these changes overnight, they should begin the process now -- today is always a good day to begin! The first line has been done for you as an example.

Person/Group	Action Item	Due Date
my son	Teach him the value of service by volunteering together once a month at the soup kitchen for the next year (or if there's another ministry that would interest him more, choose something together).	May 1st

Family Relationships

Family relationships can grow very strained during stressful times. As we age, several stress factors increase including: moving, loss of spouse, tightening budgets, and more. Any one of these can affect relationships. When you add them all together, you can see that it takes a toll.

How can you decrease the stress and keep family relations more solid? There are two key aspects which can help you accomplish both: *Plan Ahead & Show Grace.*

Plan Ahead

By going through this workbook, you are getting a jump start on this. But it is important to follow-through on the items you learn here. Do not simply put this book on the shelf for future use. Instead, review the tools and action items, and commit to the dates you have set to implement your plans. It is a good idea to review the plans every few years to see if any changes should be made.

Show Grace

Despite our best intentions, plans will only take us so far. Unforeseen roadblocks can impact your family. Try to be flexible in your plans and adjust to your changing environment. Ultimately, show grace in all circumstances.

If the senior you are assisting is becoming bothersome to you and you feel like you are about to hit your limit, then take a step back. Remember that there will come a time when they will not be there to call with good news or to give your children a hug or to bake your favorite dish at Thanksgiving. Although it isn't always easy, attempt to maintain perspective even in the toughest of times and choose to show grace and mercy to your loved ones.

Or maybe you are becoming bothersome to your loved one. They wish you would "quit interfering with their life" and telling them what they "can and cannot do." Explain to them that you are doing it out of love. You are concerned for them and want to honor them by coming alongside of them as they grow older. Acknowledge their concerns and discuss your perspective. Most of the time, you can reach a peaceful agreement.

"Experience is not what happens to you. It is what you do with what happens to you. Don't waste your pain; use it to help others."

Rick Warren [16]

Aging is difficult for the parents as well as their children. The bottom line is this: *Plan ahead as much as possible and show grace to be flexible on the rest.* This will strengthen your family relationships in even the most stressful of circumstances.

Restoring Relationships

As we age, there will most likely be people in our lives whom we have hurt deeply or whom we have been hurt by deeply. For many people, it is not until the other person in the fractured relationship has passed away that they start to have regrets for not working through the conflict while they were still alive.

One of the greatest gifts you can give others is the knowledge that you are at peace with them. As much as it is within your power, make every effort to help the person or persons you are assisting to restore those relationships before it is too late.

A common theme in broken relationships is regret - whether it be regret for what happened or regret for the delay in resolving the pain. Given enough time, regret will inevitably surface. Try to take care of these regrets while you can. Regardless of whether your loved one was the person who caused the pain or if they were the person who was hurt, help them not to delay in trying to restore the relationship.

> *"Ask God to make a forgiving spirit part of your legacy, not only reconciling you with others but also passing on an example of Christ's forgiveness and grace to those who come after you. It isn't easy; it will take much thought, wisdom, and prayer. But it will be one of the most important things you ever do."*
>
> Billy Graham [17]

Forgiveness is a powerful tool, and it is one that should be used regularly.

Family Heritage

After loved ones have died, nothing is as valuable as the memories you have of them and the information that only they knew - the stories, the laughter, the difficult lessons learned, names of relatives from prior generations, and more.

Too often, we procrastinate on gathering this information because it takes time and a conscious effort to organize it. However, if something were to happen to your loved ones today, those stories will never be told. Maybe you have old family pictures of people that the next generation won't be able to identify. Take the time to get these items in order and to make multiple copies for your children/grandchildren.

Here are a few suggestions to help you capture and organize this priceless information:

1) At the next family reunion or holiday gathering, sit down with a list of questions that will get the discussions flowing. If you have several relatives together, you won't believe the memories they'll share! They often feed off of each other and it helps them recall more details. There is a list of topics/ideas in "Worksheet 1: Legacy Questions" to get you started, but not all the questions will be applicable to your situation.

> "Let us be sure that those who come after will say of us in our time, that in our time we did everything that could be done. We finished the race; we kept them free; we kept the faith."
>
> Ronald Reagan [18]

2) Make a video recording of an "interview" of your parents -- ask them questions that you, your siblings, and other relatives might want to know. You can even get others involved in this project by having them send you their questions. For example, "What was it like when you grew up?" "Where you rich/poor/ middle class?" "How did you meet Grandma?" "Was it love at first sight?" "What were your parents & your grandparents like?" "What lessons did you learn from them?" "What are some of your favorite memories?" "What was your most special Christmas ever & why?" "What was it like serving your country?" "What struggles did you face growing up? ...as an adult?" "How did you make it through the bad times?" Make a list of questions and record it. Then make a copy for each of your family members as a keepsake. Make this a family Christmas gift to each other. The more involvement, the better. There is a list of topics/ideas in "Worksheet 1: Legacy Questions" to get you started, but not all the questions will be applicable to your situation.

3) Go through the old family pictures. Scan copies so there are digital records that you can share with your family. As pictures age (especially polaroids), they grow darker, so the sooner you start this project, the better. You can purchase a scanner yourself or pay someone to scan them for you. Title the pictures so that people will know as much info as you have (who is in the picture, when it was taken, location).

4) Hire a Legacy Videographer. They will come to your parents' home or preferred location and interview them and then make a video for the family. Some will even scan the pictures and include them in the DVD so that everyone has a record of their heritage.

This is an invaluable gift, one that only you can give from your parents' perspective. So don't delay - get started soon!

Worksheet 1: Legacy Questions

Below are some questions to help you get started recording your family's legacy.

Childhood
1. What was it like when you grew up? ...in your home? ...in the nation?
2. What was your favorite childhood toy? Was it a gift? If so, from whom?
3. How did you get your name? What significance does it hold?
4. What are some of your favorite childhood memories?
5. Who was your best childhood friend? Describe how you met and why you liked them.
6. How many siblings did you have? Which one(s) were you closest to? Why?
7. What jobs, activities, volunteer work, etc. were your parents involved with?
8. What were your grandparents like? Did you visit them often?
9. Describe your grandparents' homes and give a favorite story or two about each person.
10. What scent or smell reminds you of your childhood? Why?

Young Adulthood/College Years
1. What chores did you do growing up? Did you like any of them? Why or why not?
2. Did you have a pet? Describe how you got it, how you named it, etc.
3. What was your favorite subject in school? Why?
4. Did you have a favorite teacher? Describe why you liked them.
5. Name and describe 1 or 2 adults who most influenced you growing up.
6. What did you want to be when you grew up? Did that change? Why?
7. What hobbies or sports were you involved in?
8. Describe your first date. ...your first kiss?
9. What mischievous activities did you do? What did you learn from them?
10. Do you have any regrets or lessons learned you want to share from this life-stage?

Family Years & Early Career

1. How and when did you meet your spouse? Did anyone introduce you? Describe your first impressions.

2. What did you do on your first date with your spouse? Describe where you went, the meal, and any other memories you have.

3. When did you know that he/she was "the one"? When/how did you get engaged?

4. What was your wedding day like? Was it an indoor or outdoor ceremony? Who officiated it? Describe the clothes, decorations, bridal party, reception, etc. What thoughts/worries/dreams did you have that day? Did you go on a honeymoon? If so, describe where and share a humorous story about the trip.

5. What apartments/houses have you lived in since you got married? What were they like?

6. What was your first job after marriage? How did your career change over time?

7. How did you like to spend your "free time"? What hobbies did you have?

8. Did you take any memorable family vacations?

9. Did you attend family reunions? If so, what were they like? Do you have any memories or funny stories to share from them?

10. Name and describe 1 or 2 people who most influenced you in this stage of life.

Mid-life/Retirement Years/Post-Retirement

1. Describe the most interesting place you have ever visited.

2. What is your favorite vacation ever and why?

3. Did anyone ever surprise you with an unexpected gift or party? Describe it.

4. What work/organizations have you been involved with? What did you like and not like about the experiences you had with each group? What lessons did you learn?

5. What have been the most important turning points or milestones in your life?

6. What important changes have you seen in your lifetime (good and bad)?

7. What would you like to see happen in the next 10 years?

8. What places would you still like to visit and why?

9. Name one thing you would still like to learn (hobby, musical instrument, education, etc.).

10. Name and describe 1 or 2 people who most influenced you in this stage of life.

Legacy and General Advice
1. What is a life-lesson you learned during a difficult time in your life?
2. What is a life-lesson you learned during a happy time in your life?
3. What would you do differently in life if you could change your personal history? What choices do you regret?
4. What difficult choices did you make that you are glad you took the harder path? What did you learn from these experiences?
5. How do you want people to remember you?
6. In your opinion, what are some of life's greatest gifts?   ...most difficult challenges?
7. What is the one item you treasure the most and why?
8. What family tradition(s) would you like to see passed on to future generations?
9. What advice would you like to pass on to me? ...to future generations?
10. What life principle(s) would you like to pass on to me? ...to future generations?

Favorite Sayings/Songs/Scriptures - List their top 10 favorites below
1.
2.
3.
4.
5.
6.
7.
8.
9.
10.

Losing Friends and Loved Ones

A hard reality of aging is that you experience loss on a more regular basis. Those who live longest will be the ones at their friends' funerals, grieving with others left behind. It is important to recognize this grief and not be consumed by it. Elderly people can struggle with depression for a variety of reasons, but watching those around them die can be one of the greatest sources of discouragement.

This reality is particularly difficult for an elderly person who loses a spouse. Allow this person time to grieve. Help them balance the need to grieve and the need to move on, but remember that each person will have their own timeline. Respectfully encourage and support, but don't hover.

Recognize that grief is cyclical and will be made evident at different times. The grieving person might think they are past the deepest period of mourning and then see a reminder of their loved one that makes them cry all over again. Lovingly remind them that God knows our grief and He bottles our tears. He loves them and will comfort them during their lonely times.

> *"Watching helplessly as a loved one's memory relentlessly fades must surely be one of life's hardest burdens, and those who endure it deserve our compassion and prayers."*
>
> Billy Graham [19]

This doesn't just refer to physical loss either. Dementia and Alzheimer's disease are heavy burdens, both to the afflicted and to their caregivers. If you are struggling with this burden, don't bear it alone. There are support groups in the community and in the church body who will come alongside those who are struggling with their own gradual decline as well as their caregivers. Visit our website for links and resources to help you research the options that are available in your area.

Relational Needs Conclusion

Here is what you should have accomplished from this section:

1) You have helped your loved ones evaluate their legacy and identify steps regarding changes.

2) You have encouraged them to identify and rectify any broken relationships.

3) You have interviewed them and recorded important family history and pictures.

4) If applicable, you have sought help from support groups / counselor / church to aid you with providing chronic care for a loved one or aid your parent as they grieve the loss of a loved one.

Now, review the items on your Action Plan and complete any follow-up needed before moving on to the next section.

Spiritual Needs

The spiritual needs of each individual will vary, but it is important to recognize that we all have these needs.

This workbook will cover a variety of issues that fall underneath the spiritual umbrella. These include:

- ❖ End-of-Life Discussions
- ❖ Preparing for Eternity
- ❖ Growing Spiritually
- ❖ Emotional Effects of Aging
- ❖ Purpose, Service, and Community

We will give you the tools and resources that you need to evaluate your loved one's situation. If you need additional help, visit our website for more information.

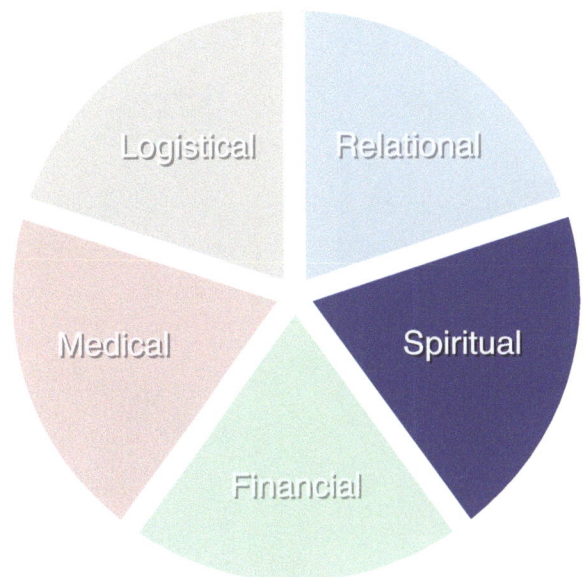

End-of-Life Discussions

In order to guarantee that your loved one's personal health wishes are carried out, they need to plan ahead for end-of-life care and decisions. It is often impossible to express those desires once a medical emergency arises, so have them put their thoughts and wishes in writing ahead of time with the help of legal documents such as a living will or a DNR ("do not resuscitate" order). These documents will give directives to the hospital and doctors who are treating them as to what level of care they wish to receive.

Having these decisions made ahead of time is **invaluable** to your family and loved ones. If they aren't, it can lead to family conflicts, arguments, and years of guilty feelings that linger long after they have passed away. Discuss these matters with them ahead of time, and arrange for them to discuss these items with their lawyer so that their desires will be carried out if the need ever arises.

> *"Christians are not to be preoccupied with death; God has put within each of us a will to survive. But neither are we to shrink from death or act as if we must fiercely resist it until the last breath. The time may well come, in fact, when life's burdens and pains overwhelm us so much that we will welcome death as a friend -- and that is as it should be. If we know Christ, we know that Heaven is our true home, and (like the saints of old) we are 'longing for a better country -- a heavenly one' (Hebrews 11:16)."*
>
> Billy Graham [20]

Preparing for Eternity

Knowing what will happen to you when you die makes these decisions much easier. If you or your loved ones aren't at peace with the knowledge of where they will spend eternity, this is **THE** most important topic we cover in this program. *Preparing for eternity outweighs preparing for tomorrow.*

The first and most important thing you can do is to decide where you will be spending eternity. It is difficult to guide your loved one in this journey if you aren not sure of the destination yourself.

The Bible says that we are all sinners and that the penalty for sin is death (Romans 3:23 and Romans 6:23). None of us has lived a perfect life. We have all lied at one time or committed any number of sins. We cannot stand in the presence of a holy and perfect God in our imperfect condition.

The wonderful news is that God loved us so much that He sent His only Son, Jesus Christ, to pay the penalty for our sins. He died on the cross and rose from the grave, overcoming death. By believing in Him and accepting His payment, we can have eternal life in heaven (John 3:16, Romans 5:8). Ephesians 2:8-9 explains that this forgiveness is something we will never be able to earn. We cannot do enough good works to make up for the sins we have committed. We must simply trust in Jesus and accept His payment for our sins. If you would like to trust in Jesus as your Savior, just talk with God about it. That's all prayer is - just a conversation between you and God. I would also encourage you to tell someone - a friend, a family member, a pastor - someone who can help you take the next steps in your faith journey.

If you want to learn more about this, we have some resources on our website to answer your questions and to guide you. If you have already trusted in Jesus but have concerns that your loved ones have not accepted His free gift of salvation, the best thing you can do is share the truth in a loving manner and pray for them. You cannot make this decision for them, but you can lead the way.

> *"You weren't put on earth to be remembered. You were put here to prepare for eternity."*
>
> Rick Warren [21]

Growing Spiritually

It is easy for people to gradually withdraw from growing spiritually as they age. Perhaps their health has declined to the extent that it is difficult to attend church or their vision has blurred so they can no longer read the Bible. Or perhaps they feel disengaged and lonely after a spouse has died or they have lost close friends.

Be aware of this and make a conscious effort (without nagging) to provide growth opportunities. That might include providing rides to church, bringing communion to them, giving them a listening device with downloaded sermons, or visiting them regularly and making Bible reading part of the fellowship time together. Perhaps a grandchild could do this after school. The important thing is to encourage spiritual growth in positive, creative ways.

Emotional Effects of Aging

Emotional effects of growing older often seep in gradually, but they can do just as much damage as physical ailments. The most common ones are: fear, anxiety, selfishness, depression, loneliness, loss of control, and anger.

If you recognize these symptoms, here are some ideas to help combat them. None of these are fool-proof and the fact is that your loved one must decide for themselves what attitude they wish to exhibit as they age. The following suggestions might help:

- Physical exercise is more challenging as we age, but even small amounts of sunshine and activity can be good for the mind and body. If your loved one is able, try to go for a walk together 2-3 times a week. Even if they are wheel-chair bound, most people enjoy being outdoors and the fellowship of having you there to talk will lift their spirits as well.

- Service to others will help your loved one maintain perspective. It is harder to fight selfishness when you are so isolated that you become consumed with your life, your ailments, and your limitations. Encourage them to look beyond their circumstances by helping others. Even a home-bound individual can write notes or make phone calls to encourage others.

> *"Has this world been so kind to you that you should leave with regret? There are better things ahead than any we leave behind."*
>
> C. S. Lewis [22]

- You will notice that we quoted the book "Nearing Home" by Billy Graham throughout this workbook. We highly recommend reading this book and giving a copy to your loved ones to read as well. Set up a time to read it together or to discuss what you have read. It will challenge their thinking and hopefully encourage them to live productive lives for the days given them, despite the physical effects of aging.

It all comes back around to showing grace. If your loved ones choose to allow their circumstances to control their decisions and their attitudes, you cannot change that. However, God still desires that we honor them. Pray for patience, and seek to show God's supernatural grace and mercy. Remember, if God grants us the days, each of us will have to struggle through the effects of growing older. Treat your elders the way you hope to be treated when you are in their situation. ***God will give you the strength.***

Purpose, Service, and Community

Encourage your loved ones to take time to consider what purpose God has for them in their later stages of life. Even if they are limited physically, there are people who need their encouragement, smile, listening ear, and their prayers. The things that your loved ones spend their whole life saying "if only I had time, I would _____." Now they have the time, so encourage them not to waste it. Try to help them focus outward rather than inward. Anytime you are successful with this approach, life is so much more fulfilling.

It is easy to get bored and frustrated with life's limitations, so anticipate this. Helping others will fill them with purpose and give them perspective. They may find that their circumstances aren't as bad as they thought when they help someone who has more limitations than they have.

> "Look for the Lord's purpose in every circumstance and in every face or voice you encounter daily, for the time He has given you is not without purpose. Prepare for each day by asking the Lord to open your eyes to what is going on around you...We can reject the opportunity to be used of God, or we can seize opportunities to impact others as a testimony to Him."
>
> Billy Graham [23]

Pray with them that God would reveal His purpose for them. Your loved one might find it helpful to talk with someone they respect about it. Sometimes a third party can objectively help them think through their strengths, experiences, surroundings, and the gifts God has given them - as well as their limitations. God will faithfully reveal His purpose for them at this time, and He will complete His purpose in them as they submit themselves as a willing vessel.

> "When I stop telling God what I want, He can freely work His will in me without any hindrance. He can crush me, exalt me, or do anything else He chooses. He simply asks me to have absolute faith in Him and His goodness. Self-pity is of the devil, and if I wallow in it I cannot be used by God for His purpose in the world."
>
> Oswald Chambers
> *My Utmost for His Highest* [24]

Spiritual Needs Conclusion

This section can be very difficult to discuss, but these are the most important topics to cover. Here is what you should have accomplished from this section:

1) You have discussed with your loved ones what their End-of-Life medical decisions are and helped them legally put those in writing.

2) You have discussed with them what happens after death and hopefully you are all at peace with those decisions.

3) You have helped them think through their purpose and decide what things they can do to serve others.

Now review the items on your Action Plan and complete any follow-up needed.

❖ Concluding Thoughts ❖

Planning for your parent or other loved one is a difficult, and often time-consuming, process. Your attitude throughout the process is vital -- it's not a chore to be dreaded, but rather an opportunity to **love** your parents through a difficult stage of life...to really *honor* them.

It's also important to share this opportunity with your siblings or others affected by the situation. There might be unequal financial ability to help, but all siblings should share equal responsibility. Each person has a unique skill set and can contribute to this process. Some are better at sitting with the loved one and discussing tough topics. Some are better at analyzing the numbers and discerning what resources are available as well as paying the bills, etc. Some have the gift of mercy and can sit by your loved one's bedside when they are sick or dying. While it can be very helpful to have one point person in charge of the planning process, it's also important to evaluate the gifts in your family and have each person contribute what they can.

If you are the primary caregiver for your loved one, here are some tips to help you maintain your own health and sanity!

1. **Educate yourself** -- research online or through books to learn more about your parents' illness. Know what to expect as their health deteriorates or improves. The more you know, the more confident you will feel.

2. **Enlist the help of others** -- don't try to do this alone!

3. **Embrace the changes** -- life may never return to "normal" and that's ok. It's important to acknowledge that and set reasonable plans.

4. **Expect to be surprised** -- after the initial crisis passes and you adjust to a new routine, don't be surprised when things happen that change that routine. Plan as best you can, but be flexible in changing those plans when necessary.

5. **Exercise regularly and eat healthy** -- maintaining your personal health is key! You can't help someone else if you get injured or sick.

6. **Encourage your loved one to be independent in every reasonable way** -- you will both appreciate this as time passes.

7. **Engage socially with others who understand** -- join a local support group; have dinner with friends; join a church or Bible study

8. **Eliminate clutter** -- the more simple your personal life, the better. It makes it easier to adjust to curve balls.

9. **Enjoy life** -- try to do at least one thing each day that you enjoy; read a book or watch a movie, etc.

10. **Equip the house to be user-friendly for your loved one** -- if they need rails for walking the hall or a ramp to enter/exit the house, invest the money to make these changes. Your back will thank you later!

Be encouraged and persevere through this challenging but rewarding process -- you can do it!

✦ Endnotes ✦

[1] http://www.census.gov/population/socdemo/statbriefs/agebrief.html

[2] http://www.cdc.gov/nchs/data/hus/hus11.pdf#022

[3] Billy Graham, *Nearing Home: Life, Faith, and Finishing Well* (Nashville: Thomas Nelson, 2011), 68.

[4] Daniel Taylor, *The Parent Care Conversation: 6 Strategies for Dealing with the Emotional and Financial Challenges of Aging Parents* (New York: Penguin Group, 2004), Chapter 10.

[5] Billy Graham, *Nearing Home: Life, Faith, and Finishing Well* (Nashville: Thomas Nelson, 2011), 62.

[6] Elder Rage, *Coping with Caregiving*, http://www.thirdage.com/today/caregiving/elder-care-startling-statistics (July 18, 2008).

[7] http://www.ownyourfuturetexas.org/long-term-care-assessment/cost-of-care/

[8] Ronald Reagan (b. 1911), U.S. Republican politician, President. Speech to Republican Party fund-raising dinner. Quoted in *Los Angeles Times* (Oct. 20, 1978).

[9] Billy Graham, *Nearing Home: Life, Faith, and Finishing Well* (Nashville: Thomas Nelson, 2011), 69.

[10] Abraham Lincoln. BrainyQuote.com, Xplore Inc, 2012. http://www.brainyquote.com/quotes/quotes/a/abrahamlin118953.html, accessed December 13, 2012.

[11] Ralph Waldo Emerson. BrainyQuote.com, Xplore Inc, 2012. http://www.brainyquote.com/quotes/quotes/r/ralphwaldo131264.html, accessed December 13, 2012.

[12] Harrison Ford. BrainyQuote.com, Xplore Inc, 2012. http://www.brainyquote.com/quotes/quotes/h/harrisonfo119676.html, accessed December 13, 2012.

[13] Dr. Kenneth Cooper. http://www.cooperaerobics.com/Cooper-Fitness-Center-Dallas/Pioneering-Fitness, accessed December 13, 2012.

[14] Mother Teresa. (n.d.). BrainyQuote.com. Retrieved February 15, 2013, from BrainyQuote.com Web site: http://www.brainyquote.com/quotes/quotes/m/mothertere133532.html

[15] Daniel Taylor, *The Parent Care Conversation: 6 Strategies for Dealing with the Emotional and Financial Challenges of Aging Parents* (New York: Penguin Group, 2004), Chapter 6.

[16] Rick Warren, *The Purpose Driven Life: What on Earth am I Here for?* (Grand Rapids, Michigan: Zondervan, 2002).

[17] Billy Graham, *Nearing Home: Life, Faith, and Finishing Well* (Nashville: Thomas Nelson, 2011), 126.

[18] Ronald Reagan. BrainyQuote.com, Xplore Inc, 2012. http://www.brainyquote.com/quotes/quotes/r/ronaldreag401608.html, accessed December 13, 2012.

[19] Billy Graham, *Nearing Home: Life, Faith, and Finishing Well* (Nashville: Thomas Nelson, 2011), 86.

[20] Billy Graham, *Nearing Home: Life, Faith, and Finishing Well* (Nashville: Thomas Nelson, 2011), 66.

[21] Rick Warren, *The Purpose Driven Life: What on Earth am I Here for?* (Grand Rapids, Michigan: Zondervan, 2002).

[22] C. S. Lewis. BrainyQuote.com, Xplore Inc, 2012. http://www.brainyquote.com/quotes/quotes/c/cslewis151465.html, accessed December 13, 2012.

[23] Billy Graham, *Nearing Home: Life, Faith, and Finishing Well* (Nashville: Thomas Nelson, 2011), 38.

[24] Oswald Chambers, *My Utmost for His Highest* (New York: Dodd, Mead & Company, Inc, 1935) November 10.

Other Resources by Mark Schupbach

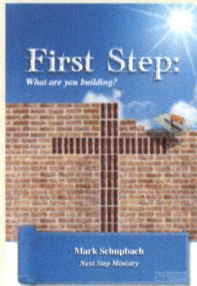

First Step: *Laying the Foundation for a God-honoring Life*

In any building project, the most critical stage is laying a solid foundation. It is the same for our Christianity, too. If we know the basics of our faith, then we'll be able to weather the storms of life.

This 10-week study is designed to ground you in those basics. Whether you are a new believer or someone who has been a Christian for years but wants to review the foundation of your faith, you will find this study to be helpful. We'll go over five topics: God the Father, The Word of God, God the Son, God the Holy Spirit, and The Holy Trinity.

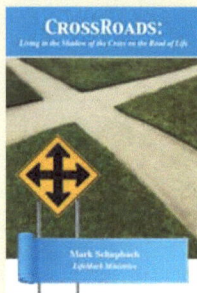

Crossroads: *Living in the Shadow of the Cross on the Road of Life*

Maybe you already have a firm foundation and you desire to live more Christ-like on a daily basis. But how do you accomplish that? How do you apply God's Word to your daily life in practical ways?

These short studies will challenge you to grow to better reflect Christ in the way you live, the way you relate to others, and the way you relate to God. These studies are grouped in topics, and each topic contains 4-6 lessons. Lessons include: Prayer, Spiritual Warfare, Anxiety, Anger, Forgiveness, Speech, Marriage, Money, Sexual Morality, Determining God's Will, and more.

Additional Studies and Resources

In addition to the above studies, LifeMark Ministries has the following Bible studies available for purchase: Genesis, Romans, Corinthians, Hebrews, and The Life of Moses.

Leadership training and materials to guide you in living a life that honors Christ are in development and will be available in the coming year...check our website for updates on these exciting programs!

Mark is also available for speaking engagements and conferences.

To find out more about these and other resources or to place an order, visit our website:

www.LifeMarkMinistries.org

LIFEMARK
MINISTRIES

www.ingramcontent.com/pod-product-compliance
Lightning Source LLC
Chambersburg PA
CBHW061055090426
42742CB00002B/44